MW01065976

Super-Mini Phrasal Verb Dictionary

Second Edition

Richard A. Spears, Ph.D.

DISCARD

New York Chicago San Francisco Lisbon London Madrid Mexico City
Milan New Delhi San Juan Seoul Singapore Sydney Toronto

Library of Congress Cataloging-in-Publication Data

Spears, Richard A.
   McGraw-Hill's super-mini phrasal verb dictionary / Richard A. Spears. —
[2nd ed.].
      p.   cm.
   Previous ed.: NTC's super-mini basic phrasal verbs. 1st ed. Lincolnwood, Ill.,
USA : National Textbook Co., ©1998.
   ISBN 0-07-149229-1 (alk. paper)
   1. English language—Verb phrase—Dictionaries.   2. English language—
Verb—Dictionaries.   I. Spears, Richard A. Basic phrasal verbs.   II. Title.
III. Title: Super-mini phrasal verb dictionary.   IV. Title: Phrasal verb dictionary.

PE1319.S63   2007
423'.1—dc22   2007016940

1 2 3 4 5 6 7 8 9 10 11 12 13 14 15 16 17 18 19 20   TRA/TRA   0 9 8 7

ISBN-13: 978-0-07-149229-4
ISBN-10:   0-07-149229-1

Illustrations by Luc Nisset
Interior design by Terry Stone

McGraw-Hill books are available at special quantity discounts to use as premiums and
sales promotions, or for use in corporate training programs. For more information,
please write to the Director of Special Sales, Professional Publishing, McGraw-Hill,
Two Penn Plaza, New York, NY 10121-2298. Or contact your local bookstore.

Also in this series:

McGraw-Hill's Super-Mini American Idioms Dictionary
McGraw-Hill's Super-Mini American Slang Dictionary

This book is printed on acid-free paper.

Contents

Introduction

Phrasal verbs, also called two-word verbs, are idiomatic expressions wherein the second element of the verb (the adverb or particle) is not necessarily predictable. For instance, why the word *up* in *call up a friend*? Why not say *call on a friend* or *call in a friend*? Actually, those are three separate, unpredictable combinations, and they each mean something completely different. For example, you can *call up a friend* on the telephone, *call on a friend* to visit a friend's home, and *call in a friend* to come help you with something.

This dictionary is a compilation of 1,800 phrasal verbs consisting of either a transitive or intransitive verb and its particle or adverb. In many cases, additional prepositional phrases are shown as part of the entry, but the dictionary focuses on phrasal or two-word verbs. This second edition of the basic phrasal verb collection is based on *McGraw-Hill's Dictionary of American Idioms and Phrasal Verbs*. The format of the dictionary is designed to provide the information needed by learners who are attempting to read and write conventional American English.

How to Use This Dictionary

ALPHABETIZATION

In this dictionary, phrasal verbs (or two-word verbs) and their related prepositional verbs are alphabetized on the verb. The variable terms (such as **someone** or **something**) are also alphabetized.

THE TRANSPOSABLE ADVERB

Adverbs in most transitive phrasal verbs can swap places with the direct object of the verb. **This cannot be done if the object of the verb is a pronoun.** Although the result may, in some instances, look like a prepositional phrase, it is not. In the following example containing "down the door," the word "down" is an adverb that stands between the verb and its direct object.

> She broke *down* the door with an axe.
> She broke the door *down* with an axe.

> Please hammer the nail *in*.
> Please hammer *in* the nail.

But you cannot say:

> *She broke down it.
> *Please hammer in it.

The entry head **break** something **down**† contains a
dagger (†) that indicates that the "down" can be transposed to a position just either the verb. Any word marked
with the dagger can be transposed to a position immediately following the verb **except when the object of the verb
is a pronoun.** Only the adverbs followed by † can be
swapped in this manner.

VARIABLE TERMS

Entries may include variable classes of words. The variable classes can be very broad, such as someone, which
refers to any person, or something, which refers to any thing,
object, or group. Many entries are very particular as to
whether they include either someone or something. Others
can refer to people or things, someone or something without
distinction. In this dictionary, these words can be thought
of as proxies for the members of the classes of words they
describe. The following examples show the kinds of things
that **someone** and **something** can stand for.

associate with *new friends* (someone)
associate with *them* (someone)
associate with *a bunch of different people* (someone)
associate with *the Smiths* (someone)
play *the radio* at full blast (something)
play *my new record* at full blast (something)
play *his huge stereo* at full blast (something)
play *all the audio stuff in the whole dorm* at full blast
    (something)

The variable classes are represented in these examples
by someone or something as in **associate with** someone or
play something **at full blast**. There are additional proxy
terms of this kind. All of them are descriptive of the kind

of words or phrases they can stand for. Here are some of the terms you might encounter.

a period of time "about an hour"
doing something "eating bread and butter"
some amount of money "about three bucks"
somehow "without much effort"
someone "Fred"
some place "the kitchen"
something "a toaster"
sometime "at noon"
someone or something which can be either **someone** or **something**.

EXAMPLES

Each sense has at least one example. In the case of the transitive verbs, the position of the adverb or particle may be either transposed or in the same position as it is found in the entry head. Learners should study the entry head, definition, and example and grasp the common elements of meaning that these three parts of the entry share. These elements are designed to share the same elements of meaning and syntax.

A

ace someone **out**† to maneuver someone out; to win out over someone. □ *Martha aced out Rebecca to win the first-place trophy.*

act something **out**† **1.** to perform in real life a role that one has imagined in a fantasy. □ *I acted out an old fantasy onstage.* **2.** to convert one's bad feelings into action rather than words. □ *Don't act your aggressions out on me!* □ *She acted out her aggression.* **3.** to demonstrate or communicate something through gestures or action rather than words. □ *Act your request out, if you can't say it.*

add (something**) on(to)** something AND **add (**something**) on**† to extend something by providing more (of something). (This use of *on* with *add* is colloquial.) □ *You added nearly one thousand dollars onto the total.*

add (something**) to** something to increase the intensity or amount of something by giving more (of something) to it. □ *You added too much sugar to my coffee.*

add something **up**† to sum or total a set of figures. □ *Please add these figures up again.*

air something **out**† to freshen something up by placing it in the open air; to freshen a room by letting outside air move through it. □ *I'll have to air out the car. Someone has been smoking in it.*

allow someone or something **into** a place AND **allow** someone
or something **in**† to permit someone or something to enter
some place. □ *Will they allow you in the restaurant without a tie?* □ *They won't allow in too many visitors.*

apologize (to someone) **(for** someone) to make an apol-
ogy to someone for someone else's actions. □ *Would
you please apologize to Wally for Tom?* □ *I apologized for
Frank to the hostess.* □ *I had to apologize for Frank.* □
I had to apologize to the hostess. □ *He was never able to
apologize to himself for his past errors.*

apportion something **out**† **(among** some people) to divide
something and distribute it among people. □ *He apportioned the cake out among the guests.* □ *He apportioned
out the applications among all those in the waiting room.*

argue someone **down**† to defeat someone in a debate. □
Sally could always argue him down if she had to.

argue something **down**† **1.** *Lit.* to reduce something, such
as a bill or a price, by arguing. □ *I tried to argue the
price down, but it did no good.* □ *Tom could not argue
down the bill.* **2.** *Fig.* to urge the defeat of a proposal
or a motion in a meeting through discussion. □ *I am
prepared to argue the proposal down in court.*

argue something **out**† to settle something by discussing all
the important points. □ *We are going to have to argue
this out some other time.* □ *Must we argue out every single detail of this contract?*

arrange for someone **to** do something to make plans for
someone to do something. □ *I will arrange for Charles
to fix what he broke.* □ *I arranged for the plumber to
install a new water heater.*

ask someone **out**† **(for** something) Go to next.

ask someone **out (to** something) **1.** AND **ask** someone **out**†
(for something) to invite someone to go out (to something or some place) [on a date]. □ *He asked her out to
dinner, but she had other plans.* □ *She couldn't go, so he
asked out someone else.* **2.** to invite someone for a visit
to a place in the country or some other location remote
from the center of things. □ *Tom must be tired of the
city. Let's ask him out to our place.*

ask someone **over** to invite someone who lives close by to
come to one's home [for a visit]. (Either to a house or
apartment.) □ *Can we ask Tom over?* □ *He has been
asked over a number of times.*

atone for something to make amends for an error. □ *You
must atone for the bad things you have done.*

auction something **off**† to sell something [to the highest
bidder] at an auction. □ *He auctioned his home off.* □
He auctioned off his home.

average something **up**† to calculate the average of a set of
figures. □ *Please add these figures and average them up.*
□ *Please average up all the monthly expenses for the previous year.*

B

back someone or something **out**[†] **(from** something**)** to back someone or something out of something. ☐ *Judy backed out the car from the parking place.* ☐ *She backed it out from its space.*

back someone or something **out of** something AND **back** someone or something **out**[†] to guide or move someone or something backward out of something or some place. ☐ *Judy backed the car out of the garage.* ☐ *Please back out the car.*

back someone or something **up to** someone or something AND **back** someone or something **up**[†] to guide or move someone or something backward to someone or something. ☐ *She backed the car up to the end of the street.* ☐ *Using hand signals, Todd helped back Mary up to the gas pump.*

back someone **up**[†] to provide someone with help in reserve; to support someone. ☐ *Don't worry. I will back you up when you need me.* ☐ *Will you please back up Nancy over the weekend?*

back something **up**[†] **1.** *Lit.* to drive a car backward. ☐ *Will you back your car up a little?* ☐ *I will back up the car.* **2.** *Lit.* to cause objects to obstruct a pathway or channel and cause a slowdown in the flow. ☐ *The wreck backed the cars up for a long way.* ☐ *Some dead branches and leaves backed the sewer up.* **3.** *Fig.* to give additional support or evidence about something. (To support or strengthen the facts.) □ *That backs up my story, all right.*

bail someone or something **out**† *Fig.* to rescue someone or something from trouble or difficulty. (Based on **bail** someone **out of jail**.) □ *The proposed law was in trouble, but Senator Todd bailed out the bill at the last minute.*

bail someone **out of jail** AND **bail** someone **out**† **1.** *Lit.* to deposit a sum of money that allows someone to get out of jail while waiting for a trial. □ *John was in jail. I had to go down to the police station to bail him out.* □ *I need some cash to bail out a friend!* **2.** *Fig.* to help someone who is having difficulties. □ *When my brother went broke, I had to bail him out with a loan.*

bail something **out**† **1.** to remove water from the bottom of a boat by dipping or scooping. □ *Tom has to bail the boat out before we get in.* □ *You should always bail out a boat before using it.* **2.** to empty a boat of accumulated water. □ *Would you bail this boat out?* □ *I will bail out the boat.*

ball someone or something **up**† to interfere with someone or something; to mess someone or something up. □ *Who balled this television up?*

ball something **up**† to roll something up into a ball. (Alluding to something, such as rope, being tangled up and so useless.) □ *She balled the clay up and stuck it to the clown's face as a nose.*

bandage someone or something **up**† to wrap bandages on someone or on someone's wounds. □ *We should bandage the wounds up first.* □ *We should bandage up the wounds first.* □ *I have to bandage him up before we can move him.*

5

bandy something **about**† to spread something, such as someone's good name, around in an unfavorable context; to toss words around in a gossipy fashion. (*Bandy* means to toss or hit something back and forth.) □ *Just stop bandying words about and start telling the truth!*

bang someone or something **around**† to knock someone or something about; to beat or strike someone or something. □ *Let's bang him around a little and see if that will change his mind.* □ *Why are you banging around my friend?* □ *Don't bang those pans around.*

bang someone **up**† to beat someone up; to assault someone; to damage someone. □ *The crooks banged him up a little bit.* □ *The crash banged up the passengers in the car.*

bang something **in**† to crush something; to dent or collapse something. □ *Who banged the side of the washing machine in?*

bang something **out**† to play something on the piano, loudly, banging on the keys; to type something on a keyboard by pounding on the keys. □ *Let me bang this melody out and see if you can guess who wrote it.* □ *Please bang out the school song good and loud.*

bang something **up**† to crash or wreck something; to damage something. □ *Don't bang my best skillet up!*

bank something **up**† **(against** something**) 1.** to heap or mound up something so that it presses against something. □ *Walter banked the coals up against the side of the furnace.* □ *He banked up the coals against the side.* **2.** to heap or mound up something to guard against something. □ *They had to build barriers to hide behind. They banked dirt and rubble up against the oncoming attackers.*

bark something out at someone

bark something **out at** someone AND **bark** something **at** someone; **bark** something **to** someone; **bark** something **out**† (**to** someone) *Fig.* to say something harshly to someone. □ *The sergeant barked the orders out at the recruits.* □ *He barked an order at his staff.* □ *The teacher barked a reprimand out to the class.*

barter something **away**† to trade something away; to lose something of value in a trade. □ *Don't barter my car away!* □ *Don't barter away anything of such high value.*

barter something **off**† to get rid of something by trading it for something else. □ *See if you can barter that old desk off.*

bash someone or something **around**† to treat someone or something roughly (physically or figuratively); to beat on or abuse someone or something (physically or otherwise). □ *Stop bashing me around, and let's talk.*

bash something **in**† to crush something inward or to the inside. □ *Don't bash the door in!*

bash something **up**† to crash something; to strike something and damage it. □ *She bashed the car up badly.*

bat something **around**† **1.** *Lit.* to knock something around with a bat or something similar. □ *Let's bat around some balls before we go home.* **2.** *Fig.* to discuss something back and forth. □ *Let's bat this around a little bit tomorrow at our meeting.*

batter someone or something **up**† to damage or harm someone or something. □ *Max threatened to batter Lefty up within an inch of his life.* □ *Who battered up this desk?*

batter something **down**† to smash or break down something, such as a wall, door, or any defensive structure. □ *Do they have to batter anything down as part of the construction project?*

battle something **out**† **1.** *Lit.* to fight about something to a conclusion. □ *They battled the matter out and came to an agreement.* □ *The two young toughs went into the alley to battle out their differences.* **2.** *Fig.* to argue something to a conclusion; to struggle to reach a conclusion. □ *The Senate and the House disagree on the bill, so they will have to battle a compromise out.*

bawl someone **out**† to scold someone in a loud voice. □ *The teacher bawled the student out for arriving late.*

bear someone **up**† to sustain or encourage someone. □ *Your encouragement bore me up through a very hard time.* □ *I will bear up the widow through the funeral service as well as I can.*

bear someone or something **up**† to hold someone or something up; to support someone or something. □ *Will this bench bear me up?* □ *This bench is so sturdy it would bear up an elephant.*

bear something **out**† [for facts or evidence] to support or confirm a story or explanation. □ *The facts don't bear this out.* □ *Her story bears out exactly what you said.*

beat one's **brains out**† **(to do something)** to try very hard to do something. □ *If you think I'm going to beat my brains out to do this, you are crazy.* □ *I beat out my brains to do this for you!*

beat oneself **up** *Fig.* to be overly critical of one's behavior or actions; to punish oneself with guilt and remorse over past actions. (Not a physical beating. Fixed order.) □ *It's over and done with. There's no need to beat yourself up.*

beat someone **down**† *Fig.* to defeat or demoralize someone. □ *The constant bombing finally beat them down.* □ *The attackers beat down the defenders.*

beat someone or something **back**† to drive someone or something back to where it came from. □ *We beat them back to where they were before the war started.* □ *The army beat back the defenders and saved the town.*

beat someone or something **off**† to drive someone or something away by beating. □ *They beat the enemy off.* □ *The army beat off the savage attack, saving the town.* □ *I was able to beat off the intruder.*

beat someone or something **out**† to beat someone or something; to win over someone or something. □ *The other team beat us out readily.* □ *They beat out every other team in the league, too.*

beat someone **out**† to outdistance someone; to perform better than someone. □ *We have to beat the other company out, and then we'll have the contract.* □ *I beat out Walter in the foot race.*

beat someone **up**† to harm or subdue a person by striking him. □ *The robber beat me up and took my money.*

beat something **down**† **1.** to break something in; to break through something. □ *Don't beat the door down! I'm coming!* □ *Please don't beat down the door!* **2.** to flatten something. □ *Sam beat the veal down to the thickness of a half an inch.*

beat something **into** someone AND **beat** something **in**† *Fig.* to use physical abuse to get someone to learn something; to work very hard to get someone to learn something. (Beating something into someone or someone's head.) □ *Do I have to beat this into your head? Why can't you learn?* □ *Why do I have to beat in this information?*

beat something **up**† **1.** to whip up something, such as an egg. □ *Beat the egg up and pour it in the skillet.* **2.** to ruin something; to damage something. □ *The banging of the door has really beat this wall up.*

bed (someone or something) **down**† (some place) to put someone or something into a bed or on bedding some place. □ *We bedded the kids down on mattresses on the floor.*

beef something **up**† to add strength or substance to something. □ *Let's beef this music up with a little more on the drums.* □ *They beefed up the offer with another thousand dollars.*

beg something **off**† to decline an invitation politely. □ *She begged the trip to the zoo off.* □ *We all begged off the dinner invitation.*

belch something **up**† to cause the release of something that goes upward. □ *The fire belched flames and smoke up.* □ *The volcano belched up clouds of poison gases.*

bellow something **out**† to cry something out loudly with great force. □ *Don't just say it. Bellow it out!* □ *Bellow out your name so we know who you are!*

belt a drink **down**† *Fig.* to drink an alcoholic drink rapidly. □ *She belted a couple of drinks down and went out to face her guests.*

belt someone or something **down**† to secure someone or something with a belt or strap. □ *Please belt the child's seat down and put the child in it.* □ *Did you belt down the kids?*

belt someone **up**† to secure someone with a belt, such as a seat belt in a car. □ *I had to belt her up because the seat belt was so complicated.*

belt something **out**† *Fig.* to sing or play a song loudly and with spirit. □ *She really knows how to belt out a song.*

bend someone or something **back**† to curve or arch someone or something backward. □ *We bent the child back a little so we could examine the spider bite.* □ *Ouch! Don't bend back my hand!*

bid something **down**† to lower the value of something, such as stock, by offering a lower price for it each time it comes up for sale. □ *We bid the price down and then bought all of it.* □ *I could see that the traders were bidding down the price, but I didn't want to take the risk.*

bid something **up**† to raise the price of something at an auction by offering higher and higher prices; to increase the value of something, such as shares of stock, by offering a higher price for it each time it comes up for sale. □ *Someone bid up the price on each piece at auction and then backed off.*

bind someone or something **down**† to tie or secure someone or something to something. □ *Bind the tarpaulin so it won't get away.* □ *We will bind down the patient tightly.*

bind someone or something **together**† to tie the parts of something together; to tie a number of things or people together. □ *Can you bind together all three parts?* □ *Bind these two bandits together and lead them to jail.*

bind someone or something **up**† **(in** something**)** AND **bind** someone or something **up**† **(with** something**)** to tie someone or something up in something. □ *They bound the books up in leather straps.* □ *I will bind up the larger sticks in strong cord.*

bind someone or something **up**† **(with** something**)** Go to previous.

bind someone **over**† **(to** someone or something**)** to deliver someone to some legal authority. (A legal usage.) □ *They bound the suspect over to the sheriff.* □ *The sheriff will bind over the suspect to the county jail.*

bitch someone **off**† *Sl.* to make someone angry. (Use discretion with *bitch*, a word many consider coarse or vulgar.) □ *You really bitch me off, do you know that?* □ *That foul temper of yours could bitch off anybody.*

bitch someone or something **up**† *Inf.* to mess someone or something up. (Use discretion with *bitch*, a word many consider coarse or vulgar.) □ *Who bitched these cards up?* □ *I never bitch up anything!*

bite someone's **head off** *Fig.* to speak sharply and with great anger to someone. (Fixed order.) □ *Don't bite my head off! Be patient.*

bite something **off**† to remove something in a bite. □ *Ann bit a piece off and chewed it up.* □ *She bit off a piece.*

blab something **around**† *Inf.* to gossip something to others; to spread some news or secret. □ *It's true, but don't blab it around.*

blank something **out**† **1.** *Lit.* to erase something, as on a computer screen. □ *Who blanked out the information that was on my screen?* **2.** *Fig.* to forget something, perhaps on purpose; to blot something out of memory. □ *I'm sorry, I just blanked your question out.*

blaze up 1. *Lit.* [for flames] to expand upward suddenly. □ *The fire blazed up and warmed all of us.* **2.** *Fig.* [for trouble, especially violent trouble] to erupt suddenly. □ *The battle blazed up again, and the fighting started to become fierce.*

bleach something **out**† to remove the color or stain from something. □ *Wally bleached his jeans out so they looked more stylish.*

bleep something **out**† to replace a word or phrase in a radio or television broadcast with some sort of covering tone. (This is sometimes done to prevent a taboo word or other information from being broadcast.) □ *He tried to say the word on television, but they bleeped it out.* □ *They tried to bleep out the whole sentence.*

block someone **up**† to constipate someone. □ *That food always blocks me up.* □ *He blocked himself up by eating something he shouldn't.*

block something **off**† to prevent movement through something by putting up a barrier; to close a passageway. □ *Sam blocked the corridor off with a row of chairs.*

block something **out**† **1.** to obscure a clear view of something. □ *The bushes blocked out my view of the car that was approaching.* **2.** to lay something out carefully; to map out the details of something. □ *She blocked it out for us, so we could understand.*

blot someone or something **out**† *Fig.* to forget someone or something by covering up memories or by trying to forget. □ *I try to blot those bad thoughts out.*

blot something **out**† to make something invisible by covering it. (See also **blot** someone or something **out**.) □ *Don't blot the name out on the application form.*

blow off 1. *Lit.* [for something] to be carried off something by moving air. □ *The leaves of the trees blew off in the strong wind.* **2.** *Lit.* [for a valve or pressure-maintaining device] to be forced off or away by high pressure. (See the examples.) □ *The safety valve blew off and all the pressure escaped.* **3.** *Fig.* [for someone] to become angry; to lose one's temper. □ *I just needed to blow off. Sorry for the outburst.* □ *I blew off at her.* **4.** *Sl.* to goof off; to waste time; to procrastinate. □ *You blow off too much. All your best time is gone—blown off.* **5.** *Sl.* a time-waster. (Usually **blow-off**.) □ *Get busy. I don't pay blow-offs around here.* **6.** *Sl.* something that can be done easily or without much effort. (Usually **blow-off**.) □ *Oh, that is just a blow-off. Nothing to it.* **7.** AND **blow** someone or something **off**† *Sl.* to ignore someone or something; to skip an appointment with someone; to not attend something where one is expected. □ *He decided to sleep in and blow this class off.* **8.** **blow** someone **off**† *Sl.* to ignore someone in order to end a romantic or other relationship. □ *She knew that he had blown her off when he didn't even call her for a month.*

blow someone or something **away**† [for the wind] to carry someone or something away. □ *The wind almost blew her away.*

blow someone or something **down**† [for a rush of air] to knock someone or something over. □ *The wind blew Chuck down.*

blow someone or something **up**† **1.** *Lit.* to destroy someone or something by explosion. □ *The terrorists blew the building up at midday.* **2.** *Fig.* to exaggerate something [good or bad] about someone or something. □ *The media always blows up reports of celebrity behavior.*

blow someone **over**† **1.** *Lit.* [for the wind or an explosion] to knock someone over. □ *The force of the wind nearly blew me over.* **2.** *Fig.* to surprise or astound someone. (Fixed order.) □ *Her announcement just blew me over.*

blow someone's **brains out**† *Sl.* to kill someone with a gun. □ *Careful with that gun, or you'll blow your brains out.*

blow something **out**† to extinguish a flame with a puff of breath. □ *I blew out the candles one by one.*

blow something **up**† **1.** to inflate something. □ *He didn't have enough breath to blow the balloon up.* **2.** to have a photograph enlarged. □ *How big can you blow this picture up?*

blurt something **out**† **(at** someone**)** to say something to someone without thinking. (Usually to say something that should not be said.) □ *It was a secret. Why did you blurt it out?*

board someone or an animal **out**† to send someone or an animal away to live, temporarily. (Usually said of a school-age child or a pet.) □ *They decided to board Billy out.* □ *They boarded out the dog while they were on vacation.*

board something **up**† to enclose or seal a building or part of a building with boards or panels. □ *We will have to board this house up if we can't sell it.*

bog down to become encumbered and slow. (As if one were walking through a bog and getting stuck in the mud. Often preceded by a form of **get**.) □ *The process bogged down and almost stopped.*

boil over [for a liquid] to overflow while being boiled. □ *The sauce boiled over and dripped onto the stove.* □ *Don't let the stew boil over!*

boil something **away**† **1.** *Lit.* to boil a liquid until it is gone altogether. □ *She left the kettle on and boiled the water away.* **2.** *Lit.* to remove a volatile chemical from a solution by boiling. □ *Boil the alcohol away or the sauce will be ruined.*

boil something **down**† **1.** *Lit.* to condense or thicken something, such as a liquid. □ *I have to boil this gravy down for a while before I can serve it.* **2.** *Fig.* to reduce a problem to its simple essentials. □ *If we could boil this problem down to its essentials, we might be able to solve it.*

boil something **up**† *Rur.* to cook a batch of food by boiling. □ *She boiled some beans up for dinner.*

bollix something **up**† *Inf.* to ruin something; to mess something up. □ *Please don't bollix my stereo up.* □ *Who bollixed up the folded laundry?*

bolster something **up**† to give added support to something. □ *The carpenter bolstered the shelf up with a nail or two.* □ *I had to bolster up the door or it would have fallen in.*

bolt something **down**† **1.** *Lit.* to fasten something down securely with bolts. □ *Did anyone bolt the washing machine down?* **2.** *Fig.* to eat something too rapidly. □ *Don't bolt your food down.*

bomb someone **out**† to cause people to flee by bombing their homes and towns. □ *The planes bombed the villagers out.* □ *The attack bombed out everyone for miles around.*

bomb something **out**† to destroy a place by bombing. □ *I hope they don't bomb the village out.*

book something **up**† to reserve all the available places. □ *The travel agency booked all the good seats up.*

boom out [for a loud sound] to sound out like thunder. □ *His voice boomed out such that everyone could hear.*

boom something **out**† [for someone] to say something very loud; to shout. □ *The announcer boomed out the names of the players.*

boost someone **up**† to give someone a helpful lift up to something. □ *She boosted me up so I could get into the window.*

boot someone or an animal **out**† AND **kick** someone or an animal **out**† **1.** *Lit.* to send or remove someone or an animal from a place forcefully, often by kicking. □ *I kicked the cat out and then went to bed.* **2.** *Fig.* to force someone or something to leave some place. □ *We booted out the people who didn't belong there.*

boot something **up**† to start up a computer. □ *She booted her computer up and started writing.*

boot up [of a computer] to begin operating; to start up one's computer. □ *He turned on the computer and it booted up.*

boss someone **around**† to give orders to someone; to keep telling someone what to do. □ *Stop bossing me around. I'm not your employee.*

bottle something up (sense 3)

botch something **up**† to mess something up; to do a bad job of something. □ *You really botched this up.*

bottle something **up**† **1.** *Lit.* to put some sort of liquid into bottles. □ *She bottled her homemade chili sauce up and put the bottles in a box.* □ *She bottled up a lot of the stuff.* **2.** *Fig.* to constrict something as if it were put in a bottle. □ *The patrol boats bottled the other boats up at the locks on the river.* **3.** AND **bottle** something **up**† **(inside (someone))** *Fig.* to hold one's feelings within; to keep from saying something that one feels strongly about. □ *Let's talk about it, John. You shouldn't bottle it up.*

bottom out *Fig.* to reach the lowest or worst point of something. □ *All my problems seem to be bottoming out. They can't get much worse.*

bounce something **around**† **(with someone)** to discuss something with a number of people; to move an idea from person to person like a ball. □ *I need to bounce this around with my family.*

bounce something **off (of)** someone or something **1.** *Lit.* to make something rebound off someone or something. (*Of* is usually retained before pronouns.) □ *She bounced the ball off the wall, turned, and tossed it to Wally.* **2.** AND **bounce** something **off**† *Fig.* to try an idea or concept out on someone or a group. (*Of* is usually retained before pronouns.) □ *Let me bounce off this idea, if I may.* □ *Can I bounce something off of you people, while you're here?*

bowl someone **over 1.** *Lit.* to knock someone over. (Fixed order.) □ *We were bowled over by the wind.* **2.** *Fig.* to surprise or overwhelm someone. (Fixed order.) □ *The news bowled me over.*

box someone **in**† *Fig.* to put someone into a bind; to reduce the number of someone's alternatives. (See also the following entry.) □ *I don't want to box you in, but you are running out of options.*

box someone or something **in**† to trap or confine someone or something. □ *He boxed her in so she could not get away from him.* □ *They tried to box in the animals, but they needed more space.*

box someone **up**† to confine someone in a small area. □ *Please don't box me up in that little office.* □ *The boss boxed up Fred in a tiny office.*

box something **up**† to place something in a box. □ *Please box the books up and put them into the trunk of the car.*

brace someone or something **up**† to prop up or add support to someone or something. □ *They braced the tree up for the expected windstorm.* □ *They braced up the tree again after the storm.*

brave something **out**† to endure something; to put up with something courageously. □ *I don't know if all the men can brave the attack out.*

break down 1. *Lit.* [for something] to fall apart; [for something] to stop operating. □ *The air-conditioning broke down, and we got very warm.* □ *The car broke down on the long trip.* **2.** *Fig.* [for one] to lose control of one's emotions; [for one] to have an emotional or psychological crisis. □ *He couldn't keep going. He finally broke down.*

break even for income to equal expenses. (This implies that money was not made or lost.) □ *Unfortunately, my business just managed to break even last year.*

break out 1. to burst forth suddenly, as with a fire, a riot, giggling, shouting, etc. □ *A fire broke out in the belfry.* □ *A round of giggling broke out when the teacher tripped.* **2.** *Sl.* to leave. □ *It's late, man. Time to break out.* □ *We broke out a little after midnight.*

break someone **down**† to force someone to give up and tell secrets or agree to do something. □ *After threats of torture, they broke the spy down.*

break someone **in**† to train someone to do a new job; to supervise someone who is learning to do a new job. □ *Who will break the new employee in?*

break someone **up**† to cause a person to laugh, perhaps at an inappropriate time. □ *John told a joke that really broke Mary up.* □ *The comedian's job was to break up the audience by telling jokes.*

break something **away**† **(from** something**)** to break a part or piece of something away from the whole. □ *She broke a bit away and popped it into her mouth.*

break something **down**† **1.** *Lit.* to tear something down; to destroy something. □ *They used an ax to break the door down.* **2.** *Fig.* to destroy a social or legal barrier. □ *The court broke a number of legal barriers down this week.*

break something **down**† **(for** someone**)** *Fig.* to explain something to someone in simple terms or in an orderly fashion. (Alludes to breaking a complex problem into smaller segments which can be explained more easily. □ *She doesn't understand. You will have to break it down for her.*

break something **down**† **(into** something**) 1.** to reduce a compound or its structure to its components. □ *Heat will break this down into sodium and a few gases.* □ *Will heat break down this substance into anything useful?* **2.** to reduce a large numerical total to its subparts and explain each one. □ *She broke the total down into its components.* □ *Please break down the total into its parts again.* **3.** to discuss the details of something by examining its subparts. □ *Let's break this problem down into its parts and deal with each one separately.* □ *Breaking down complex problems into their components is almost fun.*

break something **in**† **1.** *Lit.* to crush or batter something to pieces. □ *Why are you breaking the door in? Here's the key!* **2.** *Fig.* to use a new device until it runs well and smoothly; to wear shoes, perhaps a little at a time, until they feel comfortable. □ *I can't drive at high speed until I break this car in.* □ *I want to go out this weekend and break in the car.*

break something **up**† **1.** *Lit.* to destroy something. □ *The storm broke the docks up on the lake.* □ *The police broke up the gambling ring.* **2.** *Fig.* to put an end to something. □ *The police broke the fight up.*

break something **up**† **(into** something**)** to break something
into smaller pieces. □ *We broke the crackers up into
much smaller pieces.*

break something **off**† to end a relationship abruptly. □ *I
knew she was getting ready to break it off, but Tom didn't.*
□ *After a few long and bitter arguments, they broke off
their relationship.*

break up 1. *Lit.* [for something] to fall apart; to be broken to pieces. (Typically said of a ship breaking up on
rocks.) □ *In the greatest storm of the century, the ship
broke up on the reef.* □ *It broke up and sank.* **2.** [for
married persons] to divorce. □ *After many years of
bickering, they finally broke up.* **3.** [for a marriage] to
dissolve in divorce. □ *Their marriage finally broke up.*
4. to begin laughing very hard. □ *The comedian told a
particularly good joke, and the audience broke up.* □ *I
always break up when I hear her sing. She is so bad!*

bring an amount of money **in**† to earn an amount of money;
to draw or attract an amount of money. □ *My part-
time job brings fifty dollars in every week.*

bring someone **around**† **1.** *Lit.* to bring someone for a
visit; to bring someone for someone (else) to meet. □
Please bring your wife around sometime. **2.** AND **bring**
someone **around (to consciousness)** *Fig.* to bring
someone to consciousness. □ *The doctor brought
around the unconscious man with smelling salts.* □ *The
boxer was knocked out, but his manager brought him
around.* **3.** AND **bring** someone **around (to** one's **way
of thinking); bring** someone **around (to** one's **position)** *Fig.* to persuade someone (to accept something);
to manage to get someone to agree (to something). □
*The last debate brought around a lot of voters to our can-
didate.*

bring someone **down**[†] **1.** *Lit.* to assist or accompany someone from a higher place to a lower place. □ *Please bring your friends down so I can meet them.* □ *She brought down her cousin, who had been taking a nap upstairs.* **2.** *Fig.* to bring someone to a place for a visit. □ *Let's bring Tom and Terri down for a visit this weekend.* □ *We brought down Tom just last month.* **3.** *Fig.* to restore someone to a normal mood or attitude. (After a period of elation or, perhaps, drug use.) □ *The bad news brought me down quickly.*

bring someone **in**[†] **(on** something**)** to include someone in some deed or activity. □ *I'm going to have to bring a specialist in on this.* □ *Please bring in several specialists to advise on this case.*

bring someone or something **along**[†] **(to** something**)** to bring someone or something with one to some event. □ *I brought my uncle along to the party.*

bring someone or something **back**[†] to make someone or something return. □ *Would you please bring the child back?*

bring someone or something **forth**[†] to present or produce someone or something. □ *Bring the roast turkey forth!*

bring someone or something **out of** something AND **bring** someone or something **out**[†] to cause someone or something to emerge from something or some place. □ *The explosion brought the people out of their homes.*

bring someone or something **up**[†] **1.** *Lit.* to cause someone or something to go up with one from a lower place to a higher place. □ *We brought them up and let them view the city from the balcony.* **2.** *Fig.* to mention someone or something. □ *Why did you have to bring that up?* □ *Why did you bring up Walter? I hate talking about him!* **3.** *Fig.* to raise someone or something; to care for someone or something up to adulthood. □ *We brought the dog up from a pup.*

bring someone **over**† **from** some place to bring someone from a place, from nearby, or from a great distance. □ *They brought over the neighbors from across the street.*

bring someone **over**† **((to) some place)** to bring a person for a visit to some place. □ *Why don't you bring her over to our place for a visit?*

bring someone **over**† **to** something to bring someone for a visit and a meal or other event. □ *Please bring your friend over to dinner sometime.*

bring someone **up**† **for** something **1.** to suggest someone's name for something. □ *I would like to bring Beth up for vice president.* □ *I will bring up Beth for this office if you don't.* **2.** to put someone's name up for promotion, review, discipline, etc. □ *We brought Tom up for promotion.*

bring someone **up**† **on** something to provide something while raising a child to adulthood. □ *She brought her children up on fast food.* □ *You shouldn't bring up your children on that kind of entertainment!*

bring something **about**† to make something happen. □ *Is she clever enough to bring it about?* □ *Oh, yes, she can bring about anything she wants.*

bring something **away**† **(from** something**) 1.** to come away from some event with some important insight or information. □ *I brought some valuable advice away from the lecture.* **2.** to move something away from something. (A request to move something away from something and toward the requester.) □ *Bring the pitcher of water away from the fireplace.*

bring something **back**† **(to** someone**)** to remind someone of something. □ *The funeral brought memories back.* □ *The warm winds brought back the old feeling of loneliness that I had experienced so many times in the tropics.*

bring something **down**† **1.** *Lit.* to move something from a higher place to a lower place. □ *And while you're up there, please bring down the box marked "winter clothing."* **2.** to lower something, such as prices, profits, taxes, etc. □ *The governor pledged to bring taxes down.* **3.** *Fig.* to defeat or overcome something, such as an enemy, a government, etc.

bring something **down**† **on** one**('s** **head) 1.** *Lit.* to cause something to fall onto one's head. □ *He jarred the shelves and all the books were brought down on his head.* □ *When he hit the wall of the hut, he brought down the roof on himself.* **2.** *Fig.* to cause the collapse of something or some enterprise onto oneself. □ *Your bumbling will bring everything down on your head!*

bring something **off**† to cause something to happen; to carry out a plan successfully. □ *Do you think you can bring it off?*

bring something **on**† **1.** to cause something to happen; to cause a situation to occur. □ *What brought this event on?* □ *What brought on this catastrophe?* **2.** to cause a case or an attack of a disease. □ *What brought on your coughing fit?*

bring something **out**† to issue something; to publish something; to present something [to the public]. □ *I am bringing a new book out.* □ *I hear you have brought out a new edition of your book.*

bring something **out**† **(in** someone**)** to cause a particular quality to be displayed by a person, such as virtue, courage, a mean streak, selfishness, etc. □ *You bring the best out in me.*

bring something **out of** someone AND **bring** something **out**† to cause something to be said by a person, such as a story, the truth, an answer, etc. □ *We threatened her a little and that brought the truth out of her.*

bring something **together**† to assemble things; to gather things together. □ *Thank you for bringing everything together so we can begin work.*

bring something **up**† **1.** *Lit.* to vomit something up; to cough something up. □ *See if you can get him to bring the penny up.* **2.** *Fig.* to mention something. □ *Why did you have to bring that problem up?*

bring the house down† **1.** *Lit.* to cause a house to collapse. □ *The most severe earthquake in years finally brought the house down.* **2.** *Fig.* [for a performance or a performer] to excite the audience into making a great clamor of approval. □ *Karen's act brought the house down.*

bring up the rear to move along behind everyone else; to be at the end of the line. (Originally referred to marching soldiers. Fixed order.) □ *Here comes John, bringing up the rear.*

broaden out to become wider; to expand. □ *The river broadened out and became deeper.*

broaden something **out**† to make something wider; to expand something. □ *Now, broaden this part out a little, so it looks like a cloud, not a painted pillow.* □ *Broaden out the river in your painting so it looks very wide.*

brush someone **off**† **1.** *Lit.* to remove something, such as dust or lint, from someone by brushing. □ *The bath-*

room attendant brushed Mr. Harris off and was rewarded with a small tip. **2.** *Fig.* to reject someone; to dismiss someone. (As if someone were mere lint.) □ *He brushed her off, telling her she had no appointment.*

brush someone or something **aside**† **1.** *Lit.* to push or shove someone or something out of the way. □ *Don't just brush me aside. I almost fell over.* **2.** *Fig.* to cast someone or something away; to rid oneself of someone or something; to ignore or dismiss someone or something. □ *You must not brush this matter aside.*

brush something **down**† to clean and groom fur or fabric by brushing. □ *Why don't you brush your coat down? It's very linty.*

bubble over 1. *Lit.* [for boiling or effervescent liquid] to spill or splatter over the edge of its container. □ *The pot bubbled over and put out the flame on the stove.* **2.** *Fig.* [for someone] to be so happy and merry that the joy "spills over" onto other people. □ *She was just bubbling over, she was so happy.*

buckle someone **in**† to attach someone securely with a vehicle's seat belts. (This includes airplane seat belts.) □ *Don't forget to buckle the children in.*

buckle under 1. *Lit.* [for something] to collapse. □ *With heavy trucks on it, the bridge buckled under.* **2.** *Fig.* [for someone] to collapse or give in under the burden of heavy demands or great anxiety. □ *With so much to worry about, she buckled under.*

bud out [for a flowering plant or tree] to develop buds. □ *How early in the spring do the trees bud out around here?*

buddy up (to someone) to become overly familiar or friendly with someone. □ *Don't try to buddy up to me now. It won't do any good.*

build someone **into** something AND **build** someone **in**[†] to make a person an integral part of an organization or a plan. □ *The mayor built his cronies into the organizational structure of the town.*

build someone or something **up**[†] **1.** *Lit.* to make someone or something bigger or stronger. □ *Tom is lifting weights to build himself up for basketball.* □ *Tom needs to build up his upper body.* **2.** *Fig.* to advertise, praise, or promote someone or something. □ *Theatrical agents work very hard to build up their clients.*

build someone or something **up**[†] **(from** something) to transform someone or something from a lowly start to a higher state. □ *I built up this business from nothing.*

build someone or something **up**[†] **(into** someone or something) to develop or advance someone or something into a particular [desirable] kind of person or thing. □ *The publicity people built her up into a singer whom everyone looked forward to hearing.*

build someone **up**[†] **(for** something) *Fig.* to prepare someone for something; to bring a person into a state of mind to accept some information. □ *We built them up for the challenge they were to face.*

build something **into** something AND **build** something **in**[†] **1.** to integrate a piece of furniture or an appliance into a building's construction. □ *We will build this cupboard into the wall about here.* □ *We are going to build in a chest of drawers.* **2.** to make a particular quality a basic part of something. □ *We build quality into our cars before we put our name on them.* **3.** to make a special restriction or specification a part of the plan of something. □ *I built the restriction into our agreement.*

build something **up**† **1.** *Lit.* to add buildings to an area of land or a neighborhood. □ *They are really building this area up. There is no more open space.* **2.** *Fig.* to develop, accumulate, or increase something, such as wealth, business, goodwill, etc. □ *I built this business up through hard work and hope.* **3.** *Fig.* to praise or exalt something; to exaggerate the virtues of something. □ *The master of ceremonies built the act up so much that everyone was disappointed when they saw it.*

build up to increase; to develop. □ *The storm clouds are building up. Better close the windows.*

bump someone **off**† AND **knock** someone **off**† *Sl.* to kill someone. □ *They tried to bump her off, but she was too clever and got away.*

bump someone or something **up**† **1.** *Lit.* to damage or batter someone or something. □ *The crash into the wall bumped the race driver up a little.* **2.** *Fig.* to raise someone or something to a higher category or level. (As if pushing someone into a higher category.) □ *I wanted to fly first-class, but they wouldn't bump me up.*

bunch up to pack together or cluster. □ *Spread out. Don't bunch up!*

bundle (oneself) **up** (**against** something) to wrap oneself up in protective clothing or bedding as protection against the cold. □ *Please bundle yourself up against the frigid wind.*

bundle someone **off**† (**to** some place) *Fig.* to send someone, usually a child, somewhere. □ *Robert bundled the children off to school.*

bundle someone **up**[†] (**against** something) to wrap someone up in protective clothing or bedding against the cold. □ *Wally bundled Billy up against the winter storm.*

bundle someone **up**[†] (**in** something) to wrap someone up in protective clothing or bedding. □ *Bill bundled Billy up in his parka.*

bundle something **off**[†] (**to** someone or some place) to send something off in a bundle to someone. □ *He bundled his laundry off to his mother, who would wash it for him.*

bung something **in**[†] to cram or bang something into something. □ *He bunged the cork into the barrel.*

bung something **up**[†] to damage someone or something by blows. □ *Don't let the watermelon roll around in the trunk of your car. You don't want to bung it up.*

bungle something **up**[†] to botch something; to mess something up. □ *Please don't bungle this job up.*

buoy someone or something **up**[†] to keep someone or something afloat. □ *Use this cushion to buoy yourself up.* □ *The log buoyed up the swimmer until help came.*

burn away 1. [for something] to burn until there is no more of it. □ *All the oil burned away.* **2.** for something to keep on burning. □ *The little fire burned away brightly, warming the tiny room.*

burn down 1. [for a building] to be destroyed by fire. □ *The barn burned down.* □ *There was a fire, and the old factory was burned down.* **2.** [for a fire] to burn and dwindle away. □ *The flame burned down and then went out.*

burn (oneself) out *Fig.* to do something so long and so intensely that one gets sick and tired of doing it. (See also **burn** someone **out**.) □ *I burned myself out as a com-*

petitive swimmer. I just cannot stand to practice any-more.

burn someone **down**† *Sl.* to humiliate someone. □ *You just want to burn down everybody to make yourself seem better.*

burn someone **out**† *Fig.* to wear someone out; to make someone ineffective through overuse. □ *The continuous problems burned out the office staff in a few months.*

burn someone **up**† **1.** *Lit.* to destroy someone by fire. □ *The house fire burned the victims up.* **2.** *Fig.* to make someone very angry; to make someone endure the "heat" of rage. □ *You really burn me up! I'm very angry at you!*

burn something **down**† [for a fire] to destroy a building completely. □ *The fire burned the barn down.*

burn something **into** something AND **burn** something **in**† **1.** *Lit.* to engrave, brand, or etch marks or letters into something by the use of great heat. □ *She burned her initials into the handle of the umbrella.* **2.** *Fig.* to implant something firmly in someone's head, brain, memory, etc. □ *She burned the information into her head.*

burn something **off** something AND **burn** something **off**† to cause excess volatile or flammable substance to burn until there is no more of it. □ *We burnt the gasoline off the water's surface.*

burn something **out**† **1.** to burn away the inside of something, getting rid of excess deposits. □ *The mechanic burned the carbon out of the manifold.* **2.** to wear out an electrical or electronic device through overuse. □ *Turn it off. You're going to burn the motor out!*

burn something **up**† to destroy something by fire; [for fire] to consume something. □ *Take this cardboard and burn it up.*

bust someone **out of** some place AND **bust** someone **out**† **1.** *Sl.* to help someone escape from prison. (*Bust* is a nonstandard form of *burst* meaning 'break' here.) □ *Lefty did not manage to bust Max out of prison.* **2.** *Sl.* to expel or force someone to withdraw from school. (*Bust* is a nonstandard form of *burst* meaning 'break' here.) □ *The dean finally busted Bill out of school.*

bust someone **up**† **1.** *Sl.* to cause lovers to separate; to break up a pair of lovers, including married persons. (*Bust* is a nonstandard form of *burst* meaning 'break (apart)' here.) □ *Mary busted Terri and John up.* **2.** *Sl.* to beat someone up; to batter someone. (*Bust* is a nonstandard form of *burst* meaning 'hit' here.) □ *You want me to bust you up?*

bust something **up**† **1.** *Inf.* to break or ruin something; to break something into smaller pieces. (*Bust* is a nonstandard form of *burst* meaning 'break' here.) □ *Who busted this plate up?* **2.** *Sl.* to ruin a marriage by coming between the married people. (*Bust* is a nonstandard form of *burst* meaning 'break' here.) □ *He busted their marriage up by starting rumors about Maggie.*

bustle someone **off**† to help someone leave; to send someone out or away. □ *The cops bustled the crook off.*

butter someone **up**† AND **butter up to** someone to flatter someone; to treat someone especially nicely in hopes of receiving special favors. □ *A student tried to butter the teacher up.* □ *She buttered up the teacher again.*

button something **down**† to fasten something down with buttons. □ *Button your collar down. You look too casually dressed.*

button something **up**† to fasten something with buttons. □ *Button your shirt up, please.*

buttress something **up**† **1.** *Lit.* to brace something; to provide architectural support for something. □ *We have to buttress up this part of the wall while we work on it.* **2.** *Fig.* to provide extra support, often financial support, for something. □ *We rounded up some money to buttress the company up through the sales slump.*

buy someone **off**† to bribe someone to ignore what one is doing wrong. □ *Do you think you can buy her off?*

buy someone or something **out**† to purchase full ownership of something from someone or a group. □ *We liked the company, so we borrowed a lot of money and bought it out.*

buy something **back**† **(from** someone**)** to repurchase something that one has previously sold from the person who bought it. □ *Can I buy it back from you? I have decided I need it.*

buy something **out**† to buy all that is available of a particular item. □ *The kids came in and bought all our bubble gum out.*

buy something **up**† to buy all of something; to buy the entire supply of something. □ *He bought the oranges up from all the groves.*

C

cage someone or something **in**[†] **1.** *Lit.* to enclose someone or something in a cage. □ *We caged the monkey in, but it threw a fit.* **2.** *Fig.* to confine someone or something. □ *The health authorities virtually caged in the quarantined population until they could all be tested.*

cage someone or something **up**[†] **(in** something**)** to enclose or confine someone or something in something or someplace. □ *They caged the lions up in strong containers for the trip across country.*

calculate something **into** something AND **calculate** something **in**[†] to include something in one's calculations. □ *Did you calculate the cost of the cake into the total?*

call in (to some place**)** to telephone to some central place, such as one's place of work, as to check for messages. □ *I have to call in to the office at noon.*

call someone **away**[†] **(from** something**)** to ask someone to come away from some place or from doing something. □ *The boss called Kathy away from her office.* □ *The principal called away the teacher from the classroom.*

call someone **back**[†] **1.** to call someone again on the telephone. □ *Since she is not there, I will call her back in half an hour.* **2.** to return a telephone call to a person who had called earlier. □ *I got his message; I will call him back tomorrow.*

call someone **down**† to reprimand a person; to **bawl** someone **out**. □ *The teacher had to call down Sally in front of everybody.*

call someone **forth**† to call to someone to come out or come forward. □ *The principal called Wally forth.*

call someone **in**† **(for** something**) 1.** to request that someone come to have a talk. □ *The manager called Karen in for a private meeting.* **2.** to request a consultation with a specialist in some field. (The person called probably will not "come in," but will work at another place.) □ *We will have to call a heart specialist in for a consultation.*

call someone or an animal **off** someone or something AND **call** someone or an animal **off**† to request that someone or an animal stop bothering or pursuing someone or something; to call a halt to an attack by someone or an animal. □ *Please call your dogs off my brother.*

call someone or something **back**† to call out that someone or something should come back. □ *As she left, the clerk called her back.*

call someone or something **in**† to call on the special talents, abilities, or power of someone or something. □ *They had to call a new doctor in.* □ *Yes, they had to call in a specialist.*

call someone or something **out**† to request the services of someone or a group. (See also **call** someone; **call** someone **out**.) □ *Things got bad enough that the governor called the militia out.*

call someone or something **up**† to call someone, a group, or a company on the telephone. □ *I will call them up and see what they have to say.*

call someone **out**† to challenge someone to a fight. □ *Wilbur wanted to call him out, but thought better of it.*

call someone **up**† to request that someone or a group report for active military service. (See also **call** someone or something **out**.) □ *The government called the reserve units up for active service.*

call something **(back) in** AND **call** something **in**† to formally request (usually by mail) that something be returned. □ *The car company called many cars back in for repairs.*

call something **down**† **(on someone)** *Fig.* to invoke some sort of divine punishment onto someone. □ *The preacher sounded as though he was calling down the wrath of God on us.*

call something **down**† **(to someone)** to shout something to a person on a lower level. □ *The worker called a warning down to the people below.*

call something **forth**† [for an event] to draw a particular quality or induce a particular behavior. □ *The battle called extraordinary courage forth from the soldiers.*

call something **off**† to cancel an event. □ *It's too late to call the party off. The first guests have already arrived.*

call something **out**† **1.** to draw on something, such as a particular quality or talent. □ *It's times like these that call the best out in us.* **2.** to shout out something. □ *You should call out a warning to those behind you on the trail.*

call something **up**† to summon information from a computer. □ *With a few strokes on the computer keyboard, Sally called up the figures she was looking for.*

call the dogs off† **1.** *Lit.* to order hunting or watchdogs to abandon their quarry. □ *The robber gave up and the* *guard called the dogs off.* **2.** *Fig.* to stop threatening, chasing, or hounding [a person]. □ *Tell the sheriff to call off the dogs. We caught the robber.*

calm someone or an animal **down**† to cause someone or an animal to be less active, upset, or unsettled. □ *Please try to calm yourself down!*

camp out to live out of doors temporarily in a tent or camping vehicle, as on a vacation or special camping trip.

cancel each other out† [for the opposite effects of two things] to balance each other. □ *The cost of the meal you bought and what I owed you cancel each other out, so we're even.*

cancel someone **out of** something AND **cancel** someone **out**† **1.** to eliminate someone from something (as from a list of names). □ *We canceled out all the people who did not show up.* **2.** *Sl.* to eliminate someone; to kill someone. □ *The drug lord threatened to cancel out his former partner for testifying against him.*

cancel something **out**† to balance the effects of something. □ *Sending flowers might cancel the bad feelings out.*

carry someone **along**† **(with** someone**)** [for someone's enthusiasm or power] to affect other people and persuade them. □ *The excitement of the play carried the audience along with the actors.*

carry someone **along**† **(with** something**)** [for something] to transport someone as it moves along. □ *The flood carried us along with the debris.*

carry someone **around**† **(with** oneself**) 1.** *Lit.* to be the source of transport for someone, usually a child. □ *I'm tired of carrying this baby around with me everywhere. Can't I buy a baby carriage?* **2.** *Fig.* to have in mind the memory or a sense of presence of another person with oneself. □ *I have been carrying my dead grandfather around with me for years.*

carry someone **away**[†] [for someone or something] to cause a person to lose control. □ *The excitement of the parade carried us all away.*

carry someone or something **away**[†] to take or steal someone or something. □ *Someone carried our lawn furniture away while we were on vacation.*

carry someone or something **off**[†] to take or steal someone or something. □ *The kidnappers carried the child off.*

carry someone or something **out**[†] to lift up and move someone or something out. □ *Help me carry the baby and her things out.*

carry someone **through (something)** to sustain someone (as someone's expenses or needs) during something. □ *Can this amount carry you through the week?*

carry something **along**[†] **(with** someone**)** to bring or take something with one; to have something with one and have it handy at all times. □ *You should carry this emergency phone list along with you whenever you travel.*

carry something **around**[†] **(with** one**)** to have something on one's person at all times. □ *He carries a backpack around with him.*

carry something **back**[†] to take something back to where it came from. □ *Did you bring this here? If so, carry it back.* □ *Please carry back the empty box after you take out all the books.*

carry something **down**[†] to take something from a higher to a lower place. □ *Would you go up to the attic and carry the trunk down?*

carry something **off**† **1.** *Lit.* to take something away with oneself; to steal something. □ *Someone carried off my books!* **2.** *Fig.* to make a planned event work out successfully. □ *It was a huge party, but the hostess carried it off beautifully.*

carry something **on**† **1.** to do something over a period of time. □ *Do you think you can carry this on for a year?* **2.** to continue to do something as a tradition. □ *We intend to carry this celebration on as long as the family can gather for the holidays.*

carry something **out**† to perform a task; to perform an assignment. □ *"This is a very important job," said Jane. "Do you think you can carry it out?"*

carry something **over**† to let something like a bill extend into another period of time. □ *We'll carry the amount of money due over into the next month.*

carry something **over**† **(until** some time**)** AND **carry** something **over**† **(to** some time**)** to defer something until a particular time. □ *Can we carry this discussion over until later?*

cart someone or something **off**† to take or haul someone or something away. (When used with *someone* the person is treated like an object.) □ *The police came and carted her off.*

carve someone or something **up**† to damage someone or something by careless or purposeful cutting (of a person, can be figurative). □ *Someone carved the tabletop up. Who did it and why?*

carve something **out**† to hollow something out by carving; to make something hollow by carving. □ *Can he carve a bowl out of such soft wood?*

carve something **out**† **(of** something**)** to remove something from the inside of something else by carving or cutting. □ *She carved the insides out.*

carve something **up**† to divide something up, perhaps carelessly. □ *The peace treaty carved the former empire up into several countries.*

case someone or something **out**† *Sl.* to look someone or something over carefully, with a view to additional activity at a later time. □ *He came into the room and cased all the lighting fixtures out.* □ *He cased out the fixtures to see which ones to replace.*

cash something **in**† to exchange something with cash value for the amount of money it is worth. □ *I should have cashed my insurance policy in years ago.*

cash something **in**† **(for** something**)** to exchange a security for money; to convert a foreign currency to one's own currency; to turn gaming tokens or poker chips in for money. □ *I cashed the bonds in for a cashier's check.* □ *I cashed in my bonds for their face value.*

cast off (from something**)** [for the crew of a boat or ship] to push away from the dock or pier; to begin the process of navigating a boat or ship. □ *The crew cast off from the dock.*

cast one's **eyes down**† *Fig.* to tilt one's head or gaze downward. (Usually a sign of shame or to appear not to have seen someone.) □ *She cast her eyes down as they saw each other again.*

cast one's **lot in**† **(with** someone or something**)** to join in with someone or a group. □ *He cast his lot in with the others.* □ *She cast in her lot with the others.*

cast someone **aside**† AND **cast** someone **off**†; **cast** someone **away**† *Fig.* to dispose of someone; to reject or discard someone. □ *He simply cast his wife aside, and that was it.*

cast someone or something **up**[†] [for the waves] to bring up and deposit someone or something on the shore. □ *The waves cast the wreckage up, and it was found on the shore.*

cast something **down**[†] to hurl or throw something down. □ *She cast the glass down, breaking it into a thousand pieces.*

catch someone **out**[†] to discover the truth about someone's deception. □ *The teacher caught out the student and punished him immediately.*

catch someone **up (on** someone or something**)** to tell someone the news of someone or something. (Fixed order.) □ *Oh, please catch me up on what your family is doing.* □ *Yes, do catch us up!*

catch something **up**[†] **in** something to ensnare and capture something in something. □ *We caught a large number of fish up in the net.*

cement something **on(to)** something AND **cement** something **on**[†] to fasten something onto something with glue or household cement. □ *Cement this handle back onto the cup.* □ *Now, cement on the other handle.*

chain someone or an animal **up**[†] to bind someone or an animal in chains. □ *We will have to chain him up until the police get here.*

chain someone or something **down**[†] to fasten someone or something down with chains. □ *They chained down the bicycle rack so no one could steal it.*

chain something **up**[†] to lock or secure a door or gate with chains. □ *Please chain the gate up again when you come through.*

chalk something **out**† **1.** *Lit.* to draw a picture of something in chalk, especially to illustrate a plan of some type. □ *The coach chalked the play out so the players could understand what they were to do.* **2.** *Fig.* to explain something carefully to someone, as if one were talking about a chalk drawing.

chalk something **up**† **1.** *Lit.* to write something on a chalkboard. □ *Let me chalk this formula up so you all can see it.* □ *I'll chalk up the formula.* **2.** *Fig.* to add a mark or point to one's score. □ *Chalk another goal for Sarah.* □ *Chalk up another basket for the other side.*

chalk something **up**† **(against** someone) *Fig.* to blame someone for something; to register something against someone. □ *I will have to chalk another fault up against Fred.*

chalk something **up**† **(to** something) *Fig.* to recognize something as the cause of something else. □ *We chalked her bad behavior up to her recent illness.*

change off [for people] to alternate in doing something. □ *Tom and I changed off so neither of us had to answer the phone all the time.*

change something **back**† to cause something to return to the original or a previous form. □ *Whoever changed the television channel should change it back.*

channel something **off**† **1.** *Lit.* to drain off water or some other liquid through a channel. □ *The front yard is flooded, and we will have to channel the water off.* □ *Let's channel off the water before it gets too deep.* **2.** *Fig.* to drain off or waste energy, money, effort, etc. □ *Unemployment channeled their resources off.*

charge someone **up**† to excite someone; to make a person enthusiastic about something. □ *He reread the report,* *hoping to charge himself up enough to make some positive comments.*

charge something **up**[†] **1.** *Lit.* to apply an electrical charge to a battery. □ *How long will it take to charge this battery up?* **2.** *Lit.* to load or fill something under pressure or with special contents, such as a fire extinguisher. □ *We had to send the extinguishers back to the factory, where they charged them up.* **3.** *Fig.* to reinvigorate something. □ *What can we do to charge this story up?* □ *A murder in the first act would charge up the play.*

charge something **up to** someone or something AND **charge** something **up**[†] to place the cost of something on the account of someone or a group. (Also without *up*.) □ *I will have to charge this up to your account.* □ *Do you have to charge this to my account?*

chart something **out**[†] **(for** someone or something**)** to lay out a plan or course for someone or something. □ *The navigator charted the course out for the captain.*

chase someone or an animal **in**[†] Go to next.

chase someone or an animal **in(to)** some place AND **chase** someone or an animal **in**[†] to drive someone or an animal into a place of confinement. □ *They chased all the cattle into the corral.*

chase someone or something **around**[†] to follow someone or something around in pursuit. (There is an implication that the person or thing pursued is attempting to elude whatever is in pursuit.) □ *The dog chased us around in play.*

chase someone or something **(away**[†]**) from** some place AND **chase** someone or something **out of** some place to drive someone or something away from or out of a place. □ *The police sirens chased the thief from the building.*

chase someone or something **down**† to track down and seize someone or something. □ *Larry set out to chase the pickpocket down.*

chase someone or something **up**† to seek someone or something out; to look high and low for someone or something. □ *I will chase Tom up for you.*

check someone **in**† to record the arrival of someone. □ *Ask the guard to check you in when you get there.*

check someone or something **off**† to mark or cross out the name of a person or thing on a list. □ *I am glad to see that you were able to come. I will check you off.* □ *I checked the items off.*

check someone or something **out**† to evaluate someone or something. □ *That stock sounds good. I'll check it out.*

check someone or something **out** (**of** something) to do the paperwork necessary to remove someone or something from something or some place. □ *I will have the manager check you out of the hotel and send you the bill.*

check something **in**† **1.** to record that someone has returned something. □ *I asked the librarian to check the book in for me.* **2.** to take something to a place, return it, and make sure that its return has been recorded. **3.** to examine a shipment or an order received and make certain that everything ordered was received. □ *I checked the order in and sent a report to the manager.*

check something **out**† to examine or try something; to think about something. □ *It's something we all have to be concerned with. Check it out.*

cheer someone or something **on**† to encourage someone or a group to continue to do well, as by cheering. □ *We cheered them on, and they won.*

cheer someone **up**† to make a sad person happy. □ *When Bill was sick, Ann tried to cheer him up by reading to him.*

cheer up [for a sad person] to become happy. □ *After a while, she began to cheer up and smile more.*

chew someone or something **up**† to damage or ruin someone or something by pinching, grinding, biting, etc. □ *Stay away from the mower blade or it will chew you up.*

chew something **over**† **1.** *Inf.* to talk something over; to discuss something. □ *We can chew it over at lunch.* □ *Why don't we do lunch sometime and chew over these matters?* **2.** AND **chew on** something *Fig.* to think something over. □ *I'll have to chew it over for a while. I'm not sure now.* □ *I have to chew on all this stuff for a day or two. Then I'll get back to you.*

chew something **up**† to grind food with the teeth until it can be swallowed. □ *You had better chew that stuff up well.*

chip in (on something**)** AND **chip** something **in**† **(on** something**) 1.** to contribute a small amount of money to a fund that will be used to buy something. □ *Could you chip in a dollar on the gift, please?* **2. chip in (on** something**) (for** someone**)** to contribute money toward a gift for someone. □ *Would you please chip in on the present for Richard?* □ *Will you chip in for Randy?*

choke someone **off**† to prevent someone from continuing to talk. (A figurative use; does not imply physical choking.) □ *The opposition choked the speakers' debate off before they finished.*

choke someone **up**† *Fig.* to cause someone to feel like starting to cry. □ *Sad stories like that always choke me up.*

choke something **back**† to fight hard to keep something from coming out of one's mouth, such as sobs, tears, angry words, vomit, etc. □ *I tried to choke the unpleasant words back, but I could not.*

choke something **down**† to eat something, even though it is hard to swallow or tastes bad. □ *The cough medicine tasted terrible, but I managed to choke it down.*

choke something **off**† **1.** *Lit.* to restrict or strangle a living creature's windpipe. □ *The tight collar on the cat tended to choke its airstream off.* **2.** *Fig.* to put an end to debate or discussion; to stop the flow of words from any source. □ *Are they going to choke the debate off?*

choke something **up**† **1.** to clog something up; to fill up and block something. □ *Branches and leaves choked the sewer up.* **2.** to cough or choke until something that has blocked one's windpipe is brought up. □ *The old man choked up the candy that was stuck in his windpipe.*

choke up 1. to feel like crying. □ *I choked up when I heard the news.* □ *He was beginning to choke up as he talked.* **2.** to become emotional or saddened so that one cannot speak. □ *I choked up when I heard about the disaster.*

chop something **back**† to prune vegetation; to reduce the size of plants by cutting. □ *Why don't you chop those bushes back while you have the shears out?*

chop something **down**† **1.** *Lit.* to cut down something, such as a tree, with an ax. □ *Please don't chop my favorite tree down.* **2.** *Fig.* to destroy something, such as a plan or an idea. □ *The committee chopped the idea down in its early stages.*

chop something **off (of)** something AND **chop** something **off**† to cut something off something, as with an axe or saw.

(*Of* is usually retained before pronouns.) □ *We chopped the dead branches off the tree.*

chuck something **away**[†] to throw something away; to dispose of something. □ *Would you please just chuck this garbage bag away?*

churn something **out**[†] to produce something in large numbers, perhaps carelessly. □ *We churn toys out by the thousands.*

churn something **up**[†] to stir up a liquid; to mix up material suspended in water. □ *The oars of our boat churned the shallow water up, leaving little clouds of sediment in our wake.*

clam up to say nothing. (Closing one's mouth in the way that a clam closes up.) □ *The minute they got him in for questioning, he clammed up.*

clean one's **act up**[†] to reform one's conduct; to improve one's performance. □ *We were told to clean our act up or move out.*

clean someone or something **down**[†] to clean someone or something by brushing or with flowing water. □ *He was covered with mud, and we used the garden hose to clean him down.*

clean someone or something **out of** something AND **clean** someone or something **out**[†] to remove people or things from something or some place. □ *Someone should clean those bums out of political office.*

clean someone or something **up**[†] to get someone or something clean. □ *Please go into the bathroom and clean yourself up.* □ *I'll clean up the kids before we leave for dinner.*

clean someone **out**† **1.** *Fig.* to get or use up all of someone's money. □ *The bill for supper cleaned me out, and we couldn't go to the flick.* **2.** *Fig.* to empty someone's bowels. □ *That medicine I took really cleaned me out.*

clean something **out**† to remove dirt or unwanted things from the inside of something. □ *Someone has to clean the garage out.*

clean up (on something**)** *Fig.* to make a lot of money on something. □ *The promoters cleaned up on the product.*

clear something **away**† to take something away. □ *Please clear the children's toys away.*

clear something **up**† **1.** to make something more clear. □ *Let the muddy water stand overnight so it will clear up.* **2.** to explain something; to solve a mystery. □ *I think that we can clear this matter up without calling in the police.* **3.** to cause a rash or inflammation to return to normal; to cause skin to "clear." □ *There is some new medicine that will clear your rash up.* **4.** to cure a disease or a medical condition. □ *The doctor will give you something to clear up your congestion.*

clip something **on(to)** someone or something AND **clip** something **on**† to attach something to someone or something with a clip. □ *I clipped a little name tag onto him before I put him on the plane.*

clock in to record one's time of arrival, usually by punching a time clock. □ *What time did she clock in?*

clock out to record one's time of departure, usually by punching a time clock. □ *I will clock out just before I go home.*

clock something **up**† **1.** to record the accumulated hours, miles, etc., of some device or machine. (The recording is usually done by a meter of some type such as a speedometer, an elapsed time meter, etc. □ *She must have clocked two hundred flying hours up in six months.* **2.** to reach a goal that is worthy of being recorded. (Typically sports journalism. Compare this with **chalk** something **up**.) □ *Patrick clocked a fantastic number of points up this year.*

clog someone **up**[†] [for some kind of food] to constipate someone. □ *This cheese clogs me up. I can't eat it.*

clog something **up**[†] [for something] to obstruct a channel or conduit. □ *The leaves clogged the gutters up.*

clog up [for a channel or conduit] to become blocked. □ *The canal clogged up with leaves and mud.*

close down AND **shut down** [for someone] to close a business, office, shop, etc., permanently or temporarily. □ *This shop will have to close down if they raise taxes.*

close someone or something **down**[†] to force someone or someone's business, office, shop, etc., to close permanently or temporarily. □ *The health department closed the restaurant down.*

close someone **up**[†] to close a surgical wound at the end of a surgical procedure. □ *Fred, would you close her up for me?*

close something **down**[†] AND **shut** something **down**[†] to make something stop operating; to put something out of business. □ *The police closed the illegal casino down.*

close something **off**[†] to prevent entrance into something; to **block** something **off**. □ *Please don't close this passageway off.*

close something **out**[†] **1.** to sell off a particular kind of merchandise with the intention of not selling it in the future. □ *These are not selling. Let's close them out.* **2.** to prevent further registration in something. □ *We are going to have to close this class out.*

close something **up**† **1.** to close someone's business, office, shop, etc., temporarily or permanently. □ *Tom's restaurant nearly went out of business when the health department closed him up.* □ *The health department closed up the restaurant.* **2.** to close something that is open, such as a door or a box. □ *Please close the door when you leave.*

close up 1. Lit. [for an opening] to close completely. □ *The door closed up and would not open again.* **2.** Fig. [for a place of business] to close for business. □ *The store closed up and did not open until the next day.*

clue someone **in**† **(on** something**)** to inform someone of something. □ *Please clue me in on what's been going on.*

clunk something **down**† to drop or place something heavily on something so that it makes a clunking noise. □ *He clunked the big box down on the table.*

clutter something **up**† to mess something up; to fill something or some place up with too many things. □ *Heaps of newspapers cluttered the room up and made it a fire hazard.*

coil something **up**† to roll or twist something into a coil. □ *Maria coiled the strip of stamps up and put them in the little dispenser.* □ *Please coil up the rope.*

color something **in**† to paint or draw color on a pattern or outline. □ *Here is a sketch. Please color it in.* □ *Color in the sketch, please.*

come apart to break apart; to break up. □ *The missile came apart in midair.*

come away (from someone or something**)** to move away from someone or something. □ *Please come away from the fire. You will get burned if you don't.*

come back to return; to return to an advantageous or favorable state or condition. □ *Walter practiced every day, hoping to come back from his injury.*

come forth to come out; to move forward and appear. □ *All the stage crew came forth and received some applause.*

come on 1. Stop it!; Stop doing that. (Usually **Come on!**) □ *Mary: Are you really going to sell your new car? Sally: Come on! How dumb do you think I am?* **2.** please oblige me. □ *Mother: Sorry. You can't go! Bill: Come on, let me go to the picnic!* **3.** to hurry up; to follow someone. □ *If you don't come on, we'll miss the train.* **4.** [for electricity or some other device] to start operating. □ *After a while, the lights came on again.* **5.** to walk out and appear on stage. □ *You are to come on when you hear your cue.* **6.** *Fig.* [for a pain] to begin hurting; [for a disease] to attack someone. □ *The pain began to come on again, and Sally had to lie down.* **7.** [for a program] to be broadcast on radio or television. □ *The news didn't come on until an hour later.*

come out 1. *Lit.* to exit; to leave the inside of a place. □ *When do you think they will all come out?* **2.** *Fig.* to result; to succeed; to happen. □ *I hope everything comes out fine.* **3.** *Fig.* to come before the public; [for a book] to be published; [for a report] to be made public. □ *A new magazine has just come out.* **4.** *Fig.* to become visible or evident. □ *His pride came out in his refusal to accept help.* □ *The real reason finally came out, and it was not flattering.* **5.** *Fig.* [for a young woman] to make a social debut. (Now only done in certain U.S. regions.) □ *Does your daughter plan to come out this year?* **6.** *Fig.*

to reveal one's homosexuality. □ *Herbie finally came out when he was forty-five.*

come together 1. to touch together; to meet. □ *The ends of the boards just came together. They were almost too short.* **2.** to attend something together; to arrive at an event together. □ *Alice and I are going to come together.*

come up 1. *Lit.* to come from a lower place to a higher one. □ *Come up and enjoy the view from the tallest rooftop in the county.* **2.** *Lit.* to come near; to approach. □ *He came up and began to talk to us.* □ *A heron came up while we were fishing, but it just ignored us.* **3.** *Fig.* to come to someone's attention. □ *The question of what time to be there never came up.*

conduct someone **out of** something AND **conduct** someone **out**† to lead someone out of something or some place. □ *The usher conducted the gentleman out of the hall.*

conjure someone or something **up**† **1.** *Lit.* to make someone or something appear, seemingly by the use of magic. □ *The magician conjured seven white doves up.* **2.** *Fig.* to manage to locate someone or something. □ *I think I can conjure a pencil up for you.* □ *Do you think you can conjure up a large coffee urn in the next half hour?* **3.** *Fig.* to manage to think up or imagine someone or something in one's mind. □ *All I could do was to conjure up happy memeories.*

contract something **out**† to make an agreement with someone to do a specific amount of work. (Rather than doing it oneself or in one's own place of business.) □ *I will contract this out and have it done by consultants.*

cook (something**) out**† to cook food out of doors. □ *Shall we cook out some chicken tonight?* □ *Yes, let's cook out.*

cook something **up**† **1.** *Lit.* to prepare a batch of some kind of food by cooking. □ *Fred cooked a batch of beans up for the ranch hands.* **2.** *Fig.* to devise or concoct something. □ *Fred cooked up a scheme that was supposed to earn him a lot of money.*

cook something **up**† **(with** someone**)** *Fig.* to arrange or plan to do something with someone. (The *something* is usually the word *something*.) □ *I tried to cook something up with Karen for Tuesday.* □ *I want to cook up something with John.*

cool someone **down**† AND **cool** someone **off**† **1.** *Lit.* to cool someone by reducing the heat or applying something cold. □ *Here, have a cold drink. Cool yourself down.* □ *We need to cool off the pudding in a hurry.* **2.** *Fig.* to reduce someone's anger. (Reducing the "heat" of anger.) □ *I just stared at him while he was yelling. I knew that would cool him down.* **3.** *Fig.* to reduce someone's passion or love. (Reducing the "heat" of passion.) □ *When she slapped him, that really cooled him down.*

cool someone **out**† *Sl.* to calm someone; to appease someone. □ *The manager appeared and tried to cool out everybody, but that was a waste of time.*

coop someone or something **up**† to confine someone or something in a small place. □ *Don't coop me up. I can't stand small places.*

copy something **down**† **(from** someone or something**)** to copy onto paper what someone says; to copy onto paper what one reads. □ *Please copy this down from Tony.* □ *Ted copied down the directions from the invitation.*

cordon something **off**† to mark off an area where people should not go with a rope, tape, ribbon, etc. □ *The police cordoned the scene of the crime off, and we could not even get close.*

cough something up (sense 3)

cork something **up**† **1.** *Lit.* to close and seal a bottle with a cork. □ *I think we should cork this up and save it for later.* **2.** *Fig.* to stop up one's mouth and be quiet. □ *Cork it up and listen!*

cost something **out**† to figure out the total cost of some set of costs or a complex purchase of goods or services. □ *Give me a minute to cost this out, and I will have an estimate for you.*

cough something **up**† **1.** to get something out of the body by coughing. □ *She coughed some matter up and took some more medicine.* **2.** *Euph.* to vomit something. □ *The dog coughed the rabbit up.* □ *The dog coughed up the food it had eaten.* **3.** *Sl.* to produce or present something, such as an amount of money.

count off [for a series of people, one by one] to say aloud the next number in a fixed sequence. □ *The soldiers counted off by threes.*

count someone **in (for** something) AND **count** someone **in (on** something); **count** someone **in**[†] to include someone as part of something. □ *Please count me in for the party.* □ *Do count me in on it.*

count someone or something **off**[†] to count people or things, to see if they are all there. (See also **count off**.) □ *Let's count them off to see who's missing.* □ *Count off each person, one by one.*

count someone or something **up**[†] to count things or people to see how many there are. □ *Let's count them up and see how many we have.* □ *I counted all the guests up, and there are too many to seat.*

count something **in**[†] to include something in a count of something. □ *Did you count the tall ones in?*

count something **out**[†] **1.** to disregard something; to eliminate a possibility. □ *We'll have to count out the possibility of his being elected.* □ *Never count it out. It can always happen.* **2.** to give out things, counting them one by one. □ *She counted the cookies out, one by one.*

cover someone or something **up**[†] to place something on someone or something for protection or concealment. □ *Cover the pie up, so Terry won't see it.*

cover someone's **tracks (up)**[†] to conceal one's trail; to conceal one's past activities. □ *She was able to cover her tracks up so that they couldn't pin the charges on her.* □ *It's easy to cover up your tracks when the investigators botch their job.*

cover something **up 1.** *Lit.* to place some sort of cover on something. □ *Please cover up that mess with a cloth.* **2.** *Fig.* to conceal a wrongdoing; to conceal evidence. □ *They tried to cover the crime up, but the single footprint gave them away.*

crack down (on someone or something**)** to put limits on someone or something; to become strict about enforcing rules about someone or something. □ *The police cracked down on the street gangs.*

crack someone **up**† to make someone laugh very hard; to make someone break out laughing. □ *You and your jokes really crack me up.*

crack something **up**† to crash something; to destroy something (in an accident). □ *The driver cracked the car up in an accident.*

crank someone **up**† *Fig.* to motivate; to get someone started. (See also **crank** something **up**.) □ *See if you can crank up your brother and get him going on time today.*

crank something **out**† *Fig.* to produce something quickly or carelessly; to make something in a casual and mechanical way. □ *John can crank a lot of work out in a single day.*

crank something **up**† **1.** to get a machine or a process started. (Alludes to turning the starting crank of an early automobile.) □ *Please crank the machinery so the workers can start working.* **2.** to increase the volume of an electronic device. □ *He cranked it up a little more and CRACK, there went both speakers!*

crop out to appear on the surface; [for something] to reveal itself in the open; to begin to show above the surface.

crop someone or something **out**† [for a photographer] to cut or trim out someone or something from a photograph. □ *The photographer cropped Mr. Jones out of the picture.*

crop up to appear without warning; to happen suddenly; [for something] to begin to reveal itself in the open. □ *Some new problems cropped up at the last minute.*

cross someone or something **off (of)** something AND **cross** someone or something **off**† to eliminate a name from a list or record. (*Of* is usually retained before pronouns.) □ *We will have to cross her off of our list.*

cross someone **up**† to give someone trouble; to defy or betray someone; to spoil someone's plans. (Also without *up*.) □ *You really crossed up Bill when you told Tom what he said.*

crum something **up**† AND **crumb** something **up**† *Sl.* to mess something up. □ *Who crummed the bird feeder up?* □ *Now don't crum up this deal.*

crumble away to break away in little pieces. □ *The marble pillar was crumbling away because of the acidic rain.*

crumble something **up**† **(into** something) to crunch up or break up something into pieces. □ *Now, crumble the dried bread up into crumbs.*

crumble up to break up into little pieces. □ *The cake, which was very dry, crumbled up when I tried to cut it.*

crumple something **up**† to fold up or crush someone or something. □ *Walter crumpled the paper up.*

crunch someone or something **up**† to break someone or something up into pieces. □ *That machine will crunch you up. Stay away from it!* □ *A number of blows with the hammer crunched up the rocks into pebbles.*

crush someone or something **down**† **1.** *Lit.* to press or force someone or something down. □ *Crush the leaves down so you can put more into the basket.* **2.** *Fig.* to suppress someone or something. □ *The dictator crushed the opposition down ruthlessly.* □ *He crushed down all political opposition.*

crush something **in**† to force something inward; to break something in. □ *The beam nearly crushed Jason's head in.*

crush something **out**† to put out a cigarette or small flame by crushing. □ *She crushed her cigarette out and put the butt into the sink.*

crush something **up**† to reduce the mass of something by crushing. □ *Crush this up and put it in the sauce.*

cue someone **in**† **1.** *Lit.* to give someone a cue; to indicate to someone that the time has come. □ *Now, cue the orchestra director in.* **2.** *Fig.* to tell someone what is going on. □ *I want to know what's going on. Cue me in.*

curl something **up**† to roll something up into a coil. □ *She curled the edges of the paper up while she spoke.*

curtain something **off**† to separate something or some place with a drape, screen, or curtain. □ *We curtained this part of the room off, so please sleep over there.*

cut back to turn back; to reverse direction. □ *The road cuts back about a mile ahead, and it goes west again.*

cut off 1. to stop by itself or oneself. □ *The machine got hot and cut off.* **2.** to turn off a road, path, highway, etc. □ *This is the place where you are supposed to cut off.*

cut someone **down**† to kill someone with a weapon, such as a sword, or with gunfire, etc. □ *The bandits cut the bystanders down and fled.*

cut someone **in**† **(on** something**)** *Sl.* to permit someone to share something, such as profits or loot. □ *Max refused to cut in his partner Lefty.*

cut someone or something **off**† **(from** something**)** to block or isolate someone or something from some place or something. □ *They cut the cattle off from the wheat field.*

cut someone or something **out**† to eliminate someone or something. □ *They cut out the free coffee with lunch at the cafeteria.*

cut someone or something **up**† *Fig.* to criticize someone or something severely. □ *Jane is such a gossip. She was really cutting Mrs. Jones up.*

cut someone **up**† **1.** *Lit.* to gash or carve on someone by cutting. □ *The thugs cut him up badly, just for talking back.* □ *They cut up their victim into pieces.* **2.** *Fig.* to cause someone severe emotional distress. □ *That rebuke really cut me up.*

cut something **back**† to prune plants; to reduce the size of plants, bushes, etc. □ *Let's cut these bushes back. They're getting in the way.*

cut something **down**† **1.** *Lit.* to chop something down; to saw or cut at something until it is felled. □ *Stop cutting the banners down!* **2.** *Fig.* to destroy someone's argument; to destroy someone's position or standing. □ *The lawyer cut the testimony down quickly.* **3.** to reduce the price of something. □ *They cut the prices down to sell the goods off quickly.*

cut something **off**† **1.** to shorten something. □ *Cut this board off a bit, would you?* **2.** to turn something off, such as power, electricity, water, the engine, etc. □ *Would you please cut that engine off?*

cut something **out**† to stop doing something. (Usually a command.) □ *Cut that noise out!*

D

dam something **up**† to erect a barrier in a river, stream, brook, etc. □ We are going to have to dam this stream up to make a pond for the cattle. □ Let's dam up this stream.

damp something **down**† **1.** *Lit.* to make something damp. □ Damp the clothes down before you iron them. **2.** *Fig.* to reduce the intensity of a flame, usually by cutting down on the air supply, as with a damper. □ Please damp the woodstove down.

dash something **off**† to make or do something quickly. □ I will dash this off now and try to take more time with the rest of them.

dawdle along to move along slowly and casually. □ We were just dawdling along, talking about life. We didn't know we were late.

deal someone **into** something AND **deal** someone **in**† **1.** *Lit.* to pass out cards to someone, making that person a player in a card game. □ Deal in anyone who wants to play. □ Deal me in! **2.** *Fig.* to permit someone to take part in something. □ Let's deal him into this project.

deal someone **out of** something AND **deal** someone **out**† **1.** *Lit.* to skip someone when dealing a hand of cards. □ Please deal me out of the next hand. I have to go make a telephone call. **2.** *Fig.* to remove someone from participation in something. □ *They dealt me out at the last minute.*

deal something **out**† to pass something out piece by piece, giving everyone equal shares. □ *The manager dealt the proposals out, giving each person an equal number to read.* □ *I'll deal out some more proposals.*

dent something **up**† to mar or make depressions in something. □ *I don't want to dent my car up. It's still new.*

die away *Fig.* to fade away. □ *The sound of the waterfall finally died away.*

die back [for vegetation] to die back to the stems or roots. □ *The hedge died back in the winter but regenerated leaves in the spring.*

die down to fade to almost nothing; to decrease gradually. □ *As the applause died down, a child came on stage with an armload of roses for the singer.*

dig one's **heels in**† *Fig.* to refuse to alter one's course of action or opinions; to be obstinate or determined. □ *The student dug her heels in and refused to obey the instructions.*

dig someone or something **up**† *Fig.* to go to great effort to find someone or something. (There is an implication that the thing or person dug up is not the most desirable, but is all that could be found.) □ *Mary dug a date up for the dance next Friday.*

dig something **out**† *Fig.* to work hard to locate something and bring it forth. □ *They dug the contract out of the file cabinet.*

dim something **down**† to make lights dim; to use a dimmer to make the lights dimmer. □ *Why don't you dim the lights down and put on some music?*

dish something out (sense 2)

dirty something **up**† *Rur.* to get something dirty. □ *Those pants are brand-new! Don't dirty them up!*

dish something **out**† **1.** *Lit.* to serve up food to people. □ *Careful how you dish out the mashed potatoes. There may not be enough.* **2.** *Fig.* to distribute information, news, etc. □ *The press secretaries were dishing reports out as fast as they could write them.* **3.** *Fig.* to give out trouble, scoldings, criticism, etc. □ *The boss was dishing criticism out this morning, and I really got it.*

divide something **(off**†**) (from** something or animals**) 1.** to separate something from something else. □ *Let's divide the chickens off from the ducks and put the chickens in the shed.* **2.** to separate something from something else, using a partition. □ *We divided the sleeping area off from the rest of the room.*

divide something **(up**†**) (between** someone or something**)** AND **divide** something **(up**†**) (among** someone or something**)** to give something out in shares to people or groups. (More informal with *up*. *Between* with two; *among* with more.) □ *Please divide this up between the visitors.* □ *Cut the birthday cake and divide it up among all the party guests.*

do something **up**† **1.** to fasten, zip, hook, or button some item of clothing. □ *Would you do my buttons up in back?* **2.** to wrap up something, such as a package, gift, etc. □ *I have to do this present up before the party guests get here.* **3.** to arrange, fix, repair, cook, clean, etc., something. □ *I have to do the kitchen up before the guests get here.*

doctor someone **up**† to give someone medical treatment, especially first aid. □ *Give me a minute to doctor Fred up, and then we can continue our walk.*

dole something **out**† **(to** someone) to distribute something to someone. □ *The cook doled the oatmeal out to each camper who held out a bowl.* □ *Please dole out the candy bars, one to a customer.*

doll someone **up**† to dress someone up in fancy clothes. □ *She dolled her children up for church each Sunday.*

dope someone or an animal **up**† to give drugs to someone or an animal. □ *Her parents doped her up with medicine so she would sleep through the night.*

dope something **out**† **1.** *Sl.* to figure something out. □ *He spent a lot of time trying to dope the assignment out so he could understand it.* **2.** *Sl.* to explain something carefully. □ *He doped it all out to them very carefully so that no one would be confused.*

double over [for a person] to bend at the waist. □ *The people in the audience doubled over with laughter.*

double someone **over**† to cause someone to bend at the waist. □ *The blow to the back of the head doubled Steve over.*

double something **over**† to fold something over. □ *Double the paper over twice, then press it flat.* □ *Double over the cloth a few times before you pack it away.*

double up (with pain) to bend at the waist with severe pain. □ *The man doubled up with pain when he was stabbed.*

drag someone **in**† **(on something)** to force someone to join something or participate in something. □ *Don't drag me in on this.*

drag someone or something **down**† **1.** *Lit.* to pull someone or something to the ground or to a lower level. □ *The lions dragged the antelope down and made dinner out of it.* **2.** *Fig.* to debase someone or something; to corrupt someone or something. □ *The bad acting dragged the level of the performance down.*

drag something **out**† to make something last for a long time. □ *Why does the chairman have to drag the meeting out so long?* □ *Don't drag out the meetings so long!*

drag something **out of** someone AND **drag** something **out**† to force someone to reveal something; to extract an answer or information out of someone laboriously. □ *Why don't you just tell me? Do I have to drag it out of you?* □ *We had to drag out the information, but she finally told us.*

drag something **up**† to pull something close, such as a chair, stool, etc., to sit in. □ *Drag up a chair and sit for a while.*

drain away [for something] to flow away. □ *All the water drained away and exposed the mud and rocks on the bot-*

tom of the pond. □ *When the water drained away, we found three snapping turtles in the bottom of the pond.*

drain out to flow out or empty. □ *All the milk drained out of the container onto the bottom of the refrigerator.*

drain something **off** something AND **drain** something **off**† to cause or permit something to flow from the surface or contents of something. □ *Drain some of the broth off the chicken.*

drain something **out of** something AND **drain** something **out**† to cause something to flow from something; to empty all of some liquid out of something. □ *She drained the last drop out of the bottle.*

draw people or things **together**† to pull people together; to pull things together. □ *She drew her toys together in preparation for leaving.*

draw someone **aside**† to pull or steer someone aside. □ *The teacher drew Bob aside to have a word with him.*

draw something **out**† **1.** to make something have greater length. □ *He drew out a long strand of melted cheese and tried to drop it into his mouth.* **2.** to extend something in time. □ *Do we have to draw this thing out? Let's get it over with.* □ *Stop drawing out the proceedings.* **3.** *Lit.* to draw a picture to make something more clear. □ *Here, I'll draw it out so you can see what I mean.*

draw something **up**† **1.** *Lit.* to pull something close by, such as a chair, stool, etc. □ *Draw a chair up and sit down.* □ *She drew up a pillow and sat on the floor.* **2.** *Fig.* to draft a document; to prepare a document. □ *Who will draw a contract up?*

dream something **away**† *Fig.* to waste away a period of time having fantasies. □ *I just want to sit in the sun and dream the day away.* □ *Don't dream away your life!*

dream something **up**† *Fig.* to invent something; to fabricate something. (The *something* can be the word *something*.) □ *I don't know what to do, but I'll dream something up.* □ *Please dream up a solution for this problem.*

dress someone **down**† to bawl someone out; to give someone a good scolding. □ *The drill sergeant dressed down the entire squadron for failing inspection.*

dress someone or something **up**† to make someone or something appear fancier than is actually so. □ *The publicity specialist dressed the actress up a lot.*

drink something **down**† to drink something; to consume all of something by drinking it. □ *Here, drink this down, and see if it makes you feel better.*

drink something **in**† *Fig.* to absorb something; to take in information, sights, a story, etc. □ *Terry and Amy drove up to the top of the hill to drink the sights in.*

drink something **up**† to drink all of something that is served or that is on hand. □ *Who drank all the root beer up?*

drive away to leave some place driving a vehicle. □ *They got in the car and drove away.* □ *They drove away and left us here.*

drive back to go in a vehicle back to where it started. □ *Mary drove back and parked the car where it had been when she started.*

drive off to leave somewhere, driving a vehicle. □ *She got in her car and drove off.* □ *Please don't drive off and leave me!*

drive on to continue driving; to continue with one's journey. □ *The traffic jam is breaking up, so we can drive on.*

drive someone or an animal **away**[†] **(from** something or some place**)** to repel someone or an animal from something or some place. □ *We drove the monkeys away from the pineapples.*

drive someone or something **back**[†] to force someone or something away; to force someone or something to retreat. □ *The infantry drove the attackers back into the desert.* □ *They drove back the invading army.*

drive someone or something **off**[†] to repel or chase away someone or something. □ *The campers drove the cows off before the animals trampled the tents.*

drone something **out**[†] to make a loud and low-pitched noise; to say something in a low-pitched and monotonous manner. □ *The announcer droned the winning numbers out.*

drop away 1. *Lit.* to fall off; to fall away. □ *The leaves were still dropping away from the trees in November.* **2.** *Fig.* [for a group of people] to decline in number over time through disinterest or attrition. □ *His friends gradually dropped away as the years passed.*

drop back 1. to fall back to an original position. □ *His arm raised up and then dropped back.* □ *The lid dropped back to its original position as soon as we let go of it.* **2.** to go slowly and lose one's position in a march or procession. □ *He dropped back a bit and evened up the spacing in the line of marchers.*

drop behind (in something**)** to fail to keep up with a schedule. □ *She is dropping behind and needs someone to help her.*

drop someone or something **off**† **(some place) 1.** *Lit.* to let someone or a group out of a vehicle at a particular place; to deliver someone or something some place. □ *Let's drop these shirts off at the cleaners.* **2.** *Fig.* to give someone or a group a ride to some place. □ *Can I drop you off somewhere in town?* □ *I dropped off the kids at the party.*

drown someone or an animal **out**† [for a flood] to drive someone or an animal away from home. □ *The high waters almost drowned the farmers out last year.*

drown someone or something **out**† [for a sound] to be so loud that someone or something cannot be heard. □ *The noise of the passing train drowned out our conversation.*

drum something **out**† to beat a rhythm, loudly and clearly, as if teaching it to someone. □ *Drum the rhythm out before you try to sing this song.*

drum something **up**† to obtain something by attracting people's attention to one's need or cause. □ *I shall try to drum up support for the party.* □ *You shall have to drum up new business by advertising.*

dry out 1. *Lit.* to become dry. □ *The clothes finally dried out in the wet weather.* **2.** *Fig.* to allow alcohol and the effects of drunkenness, especially if habitual, to dissipate from one's body. □ *He required about three days to dry out completely.*

dry someone or something **off**† to remove the moisture from someone or something. □ *Please dry your feet off before coming in.*

dry someone **out**† *Fig.* to cause someone to become sober; to cause someone to stop drinking alcohol to excess. □ *If the doctor at the clinic can't dry him out, no one can.*

dry something **out**† to make something become dry. □ *Dry this out and put it on immediately.* □ *Dry out your jacket in the clothes dryer.*

dry something **up**† **1.** to cause moisture to dry away to nothing. □ *Dry this spill up with the hair dryer.* □ *Will the hair dryer dry up this mess?* **2.** to cure a skin rash by the use of medicine that dries. □ *Let's use some of this to try to dry that rash up.*

dub something **in**† to mix a new sound recording into an old one. □ *The actor messed up his lines, but they dubbed the correct words in later.*

dust someone **off**† *Sl.* to punch or beat someone. □ *We dusted them off one by one.*

dust someone or something **off**† to wipe or brush the dust off someone or something. □ *Dust this vase off and put it on the shelf.*

dwindle away (to something**)** AND **dwindle down (to** something**)** to shrink, contract, or diminish to something. □ *The noise dwindled away to nothing.*

E

ease off [for something] to diminish. □ *The rain began to ease off.* □ *The storm seems to have eased off a little.*

ease someone out of something AND **ease someone out**† **1.** *Lit.* to get someone out of something carefully. □ *The paramedics eased the injured man out of the wreckage.* **2.** *Fig.* to get someone out of an office or position quietly and without much embarrassment. □ *We eased the sheriff out of office without a fight.*

eat someone up† **1.** *Lit.* to consume the flesh of someone. □ *The big bad wolf said he was going to eat you up!* □ *The bear ate up the fish.* **2.** *Fig.* [for an idea] to consume a person. □ *The whole idea of visiting Australia was just eating her up.* **3.** *Fig.* [for insects] to bite a person all over. □ *These mosquitoes are just eating me up!* **4.** *Fig.* [for someone] to overwhelm and devastate someone. □ *The guy is a devil! He just eats up people!*

eat something **away**† to erode something; to consume something bit by bit. □ *The acid ate the finish away.*

eat something **out**† **1.** to eat some kind of meal or a particular food away from home, as at a restaurant. □ *We eat fish out, but we don't cook it at home.* □ *We may eat out a meal or two, but certainly not every meal.* **2.** [for something or an animal] to consume the inside of something. □ *The ants ate the inside of the pumpkin out.*

eat something **up**† **1.** AND **eat** an animal **up**† *Lit.* to devour all of some food or an animal. □ *They ate the turkey up, and no one had to eat leftovers.* **2.** *Fig.* to consume something rapidly, such as money. □ *Running this household eats my income up.* **3.** *Fig.* to believe something. □ *Those people really eat that stuff up about tax reduction.* **4.** *Fig.* to appreciate something. □ *The audience liked my singing; they really ate it up.*

eke something **out**† to extend something; to add to something. □ *He worked at two jobs in order to eke his income out.*

elbow someone **aside**† to push someone aside with one's elbow or arm. □ *She elbowed the other woman aside and there was almost a fight.*

empty someone **out**† to cause someone to empty the bowels, stomach, or bladder. □ *This medication will empty you out.* □ *This stuff could empty out an army!*

empty something **out**† to remove or pour all of the contents from something. □ *Please empty this drawer out and clean it.* □ *She emptied out the aquarium and cleaned it well.*

end something **up**† to terminate something; to bring something to an end. □ *He ended his vacation up by going to the beach.* □ *She ended up her speech with a poem.*

even something **out**† to make something even or level. □ *Please even the gravel out.* □ *They evened out the surface of the road.*

even something **up**† to make something even, square, level, equal, balanced, etc. □ *I'll even the table up.*

explain something **away**† to explain something so that it is no longer a problem. □ *You can try to explain it away if you want, but that won't solve the problem.*

F

face off 1. to begin a hockey game with two players facing one another. □ *They faced off and the match was on.* **2.** to prepare for a confrontation. □ *The opposing candidates faced off and the debate began.*

face someone **down**† to make a face-to-face stand with someone who eventually backs down. □ *Facing down Tom wasn't difficult for Chuck.*

fade down [for sound] to diminish. □ *The roar of the train faded down as it passed and fled into the night.*

fade something **down**† to turn down a sound. (Broadcasting.) □ *The radio engineer faded the music down and the announcer's voice began.*

fade something **in**† to bring a picture, sound, or both into prominence. (Broadcasting.) □ *The technician faded the picture in and the program began.*

fade something **out**† to diminish something altogether. (Broadcasting.) □ *At the end, you should fade the music out completely.*

fade something **up**† to increase the sound gradually. (Broadcasting.) □ *The director faded the music up and then down again before the announcer spoke.*

fake someone **out**† to deceive someone; to fool someone. □ *You really faked me out. I never would have guessed it was you.*

fall out 1. to happen; to result. □ *As things fell out, we had a wonderful trip.* **2.** to leave one's place in a formation when dismissed. (Usually in scouting or the military. The opposite of **fall in**.) □ *The scouts fell out and ran to the campfire.* □ *All the soldiers fell out and talked among themselves.*

fall over to topple over and fall down. □ *The fence fell over and dented the car.* □ *I felt faint, and I almost fell over.*

fall through [for something, such as plans] to fail. □ *Our party for next Saturday fell through.* □ *I hope our plans don't fall through.*

fan something out† to spread something out so that all parts can be seen better. (As one opens a wood and paper fan.) □ *Todd fanned the cards out so we could see which ones he held.*

farm someone out† **1.** [for someone in control] to send someone to work for someone else. □ *I have farmed my electrician out for a week, so your work will have to wait.* **2.** to send a child away to be cared for by someone; to send a child to boarding school. □ *We farmed the kids out to my sister for the summer.*

farm something out† **1.** to deplete the fertility of land by farming too intensely. □ *They farmed their land out through careless land management.* **2.** to send work to someone to be done away from one's normal place of business; to subcontract work. □ *We farmed the assembly work out.*

fasten something up† to close something up, using buttons, a zipper, snaps, hooks, a clasp, or other things meant to hold something closed. □ *Please fasten this up for me. I can't reach the zipper.*

73

fence someone in

feel someone **out**† **(about** someone or something) *Fig.* to find out what someone thinks about someone or something. (This does not involve touching anyone.) □ *I will feel him out about what he thinks about going to Florida.*

feel someone **up**† to feel someone sexually. (Use discretion with topic.) □ *I heard him say he really wanted to feel her up.*

fence an animal **in**† to enclose an animal and its area within a fence or barrier. □ *We fenced the dog in to keep it at home.*

fence someone **in**† to restrict someone in some way. □ *I don't want to fence you in, but you have to get home earlier at night.* □ *Don't try to fence me in. I need a lot of freedom.*

fence someone or something **off**† **(from** something) to separate someone or something from something else with a fence or barrier. □ *We fenced the children's play area* *off from the rest of the yard.* □ *Dave fenced off the play area.*

fence something **in**† to enclose an area within a fence. □ *When they fenced the garden in, they thought the deer wouldn't be able to destroy the flowers.*

ferret something **out**† **(from** something**)** *Fig.* to fetch something out from something. □ *We will have to ferret the mouse out from behind the stove.*

ferry someone **around**† to transport people here and there in small groups. □ *I really don't want to spend all my days ferrying children around.*

fiddle something **away**† to waste something. □ *Don't fiddle away the afternoon. Get to work.*

fight someone or something **down**† to fight against and defeat someone or something. □ *We fought the opposition down and got our bill through the committee.*

fight someone or something **off**† to repel an attack from someone or something. □ *We fought the enemy attack off, but they returned almost immediately.* □ *She fought off the mosquitoes all evening.*

fight something **down**† **1.** to struggle to hold something back; to struggle to keep from being overwhelmed by something. □ *She fought her anger down and managed to stay calm.* **2.** to struggle to swallow something; to fight to get something down one's throat. □ *It tasted terrible, but I managed to fight it down.*

fight something **out**† to settle something by fighting. □ *Do we have to fight this out? Can't we use reason?* □ *I prefer to fight out this matter once and for all.*

figure someone or something **in((to)** something**)** AND **figure** someone or something **in**† to reckon someone or something into the total. □ *I will figure the electric bill into the total.*

figure something **up**† to add up the amount of something. □ *Please figure the bill up. We have to go now.*

file something **(away**†**)** to put something away, usually in a file folder or file cabinet. □ *She filed the letter away for future reference.*

file something **down**† to level off a protrusion by filing. □ *File this edge down so no one gets cut on it.*

fill in [for an indentation, hole, etc.] to become full. □ *Will this hole in the ground fill in by itself, or should I put some dirt in?*

fill someone **in**† **(on** someone or something**)** to tell someone the details about someone or something. □ *Please fill me in on what happened last night.*

fill someone or something **up**† **(with** something**)** to put as much as possible into someone or something. □ *We filled him up with chili and crackers.* □ *We will fill up the basket with leaves.*

fill something **in**† **1.** to add material to an indentation, hole, etc., to make it full. □ *You had better fill the crack in with something before you paint the wall.* **2.** *Fig.* to write in the blank spaces on a paper; to write on a form. □ *Please fill this form in.*

fill something **out**† *Fig.* to complete a form by writing in the blank spaces. □ *Please fill this form out and send it back to us in the mail.*

fill up 1. to become full. □ *The creek filled up after the heavy rain yesterday.* **2.** to fill one's gas tank. □ *I've got to stop and fill up. The gas tank is running low.*

find someone **in** to learn or discover that one is at home; to learn or discover that one is in one's office. □ *I never expected to find you in at this time of night.*

find someone **out 1.** to discover that someone is not at home. □ *We knocked on their door and found them out.* **2.** to discover something surprising or shocking about someone.

find something **out**† to discover facts about someone or something; to learn a fact. □ *I found something out that you might be interested in.*

finish someone or something **off**† *Fig.* to complete some activity being performed on someone or something. □ *Let's finish this one off and go home.* □ *Yes, let's finish off this one.*

finish someone or something **up**† *Fig.* to finish doing something to someone or something. □ *I will finish this typing up in a few minutes.*

finish something **off**† *Fig.* to eat or drink up all of something; to eat or drink up the last portion of something. □ *Let's finish the turkey off.*

fire something **back**† **(to** someone or something**)** *Fig.* to send something back to someone or a group immediately. □ *Look this over and fire it back to me immediately.*

fire something **off**† **(to** someone**)** *Fig.* to send something to someone immediately, by a very rapid means. □ *Fire a letter off to Fred, ordering him to return home at once.* □ *I fired off a letter to Fred as you asked.*

fire something **up**† **1.** *Lit.* to light something, such as a pipe, cigarette, etc. □ *If you fire that pipe up, I will leave the room.* **2.** *Fig.* to start something such as an engine. □ *Fire this thing up, and let's get going.*

firm something **up**[†] **1.** *Lit.* to make something more stable or firm. □ *We need to firm this table up. It is very wobbly.* **2.** *Fig.* to make a monetary offer for something more appealing and attractive and therefore more "solid" and likely to be accepted. □ *You will have to firm the offer up with cash today, if you really want the house.*

firm up 1. *Lit.* to develop better muscle tone; to become less flabby. □ *I need to do some exercises so I can firm up.* **2.** *Fig.* to become more stable or viable; to recover from or stop a decline. □ *The economy will probably firm up soon.*

fit someone or something **out**[†] **(for** something**)** to equip someone or something for something; to outfit someone or something for something. □ *We are going to fit our boat out so we can live on it during a long cruise.*

fit someone or something **out**[†] **(with** something**)** to provide or furnish someone or something with something. □ *They fit out the campers with everything they needed.* □ *They fit them out for only $140.*

fit someone or something **up**[†] **(with** something**)** AND **fit** someone or something **(up**[†]**) with** something to provide someone or something with something for a particular purpose. □ *We fit the couple up with fins, masks, and snorkels for skin diving.* □ *The clerk fitted up the couple with diving gear for their vacation.*

fit something **together**[†] to put the parts of something together. □ *First you have to fit the pieces together to see if they are all there.* □ *I think I can fit the parts of the model airplane together.*

fit together [for things] to conform in shape to one another. □ *All the pieces of the puzzle fit together. They really do.*

fix someone or something **up**† to rehabilitate someone or something. □ *The doctor said he could fix me up with a few pills.*

fix someone **up**† **(with** something) to supply someone with something. □ *I will fix you up with some alcohol and bandages.* □ *The clerk fixed up the lady with what she needed.*

fizzle out 1. Lit. [for a liquid] to lose its effervescence. □ *This seltzer has fizzled out. I need a fresh glass of it.* **2.** Fig. [for an item in a fireworks display] to fail to operate properly, often producing only a hiss. □ *That last rocket fizzled out. Set off another one.* **3.** Fig. to fade or become ineffectual gradually. □ *The party began to fizzle out about midnight.*

flack out AND **flake out** Sl. to collapse with exhaustion; to lie down because of exhaustion. □ *All the hikers flacked out when they reached the campsite.*

flag someone or something **down**† to signal or wave, indicating that someone should stop. □ *Please go out and flag a taxi down. I'll be right out.*

flake off ((of) something) [for bits of something] to break away from the whole, perhaps under pressure or because of damage. (*Of* is usually retained before pronouns.) □ *Little bits of marble began to flake off the marble steps.*

flame up 1. [for something] to catch fire and burst into flames. □ *The trees flamed up one by one in the forest fire.* **2.** [for a fire] to expand and send out larger flames. □ *The raging fire flamed up and jumped to even more trees.*

flare out to spread out; to widen. (Said especially of one opening of a tube or round-topped vessel.) □ *The end of the pipe flared out to a larger diameter.*

flare up 1. *Lit.* [for something] to ignite and burn. □ *The firewood flared up at last—four matches having been used.* **2.** *Lit.* [for a fire] to burn brightly again and expand rapidly. □ *After burning quietly for a while, the fire suddenly flared up and made the room very bright.* **3.** *Fig.* [for a pain or medical condition] to get worse suddenly. □ *My arthritis flares up during the damp weather.* **4.** *Fig.* [for a dispute] to break out or escalate into a battle. □ *A war flared up in the Middle East.* □ *We can't send the whole army every time a dispute flares up.* **5.** AND **flare up at** someone or something *Fig.* to lose one's temper at someone or something. □ *I could tell by the way he flared up at me that he was not happy with what I had done.* □ *I didn't mean to flare up.*

flash something **around**† to display something so everyone can see it. (Usually something one would hold in one's hand.) □ *Don't flash your money around on the streets.*

flatten someone or something **out**† to make someone or something flat. □ *If you fall under the steamroller, it will flatten you out.*

flesh something **out**† **(with** something**)** *Fig.* to make something more detailed, bigger, or fuller. □ *This is basically a good outline. Now you'll have to flesh it out.*

flick something **off**† to turn something off, using a toggle switch. □ *Mary flicked the light off and went out of the room.* □ *Please flick the light off as you go out the door.*

flick something **on**† to turn something on, using a toggle switch. □ *Mary came into the room and flicked the light on.*

fling someone or something **aside**† to toss or sling someone or something aside or out of the way. □ *She flung aside the covers and leaped out of bed.*

fling someone or something **away**† to throw or sling someone or something away or out of the way. □ *You can't just fling me away! I am your eldest son!*

fling someone or something **down**† to throw or push someone or something down. □ *He flung the book down in great anger.*

flit about to move about quickly; to dart about. □ *A large number of hummingbirds were flitting about.*

flock together to gather together in great numbers. (Typically said of birds and sheep.) □ *A large number of blackbirds flocked together, making a lot of noise.*

flop down to sit down heavily or awkwardly. □ *Be graceful. Don't just flop down!*

flop someone or something **over**† to turn someone or something over, awkwardly or carelessly. □ *They flopped the unconscious man over, searching for his identification.*

fluff something **up**† to make something soft appear fuller or higher. □ *Fluff your pillow up before you go to bed.*

flush something **away**† to wash something unwanted away. □ *Flush all this mess away!*

fog something **up**† to make something made of glass become covered with a film of water vapor. □ *The moisture fogged the windshield up, and we had to stop to clean it off.*

fog up [for something made of glass] to become partially or completely obscured by a film of water vapor.

fold something **back**† to bend a sheet or flap of something back. □ *She very carefully folded the page back to mark her place in the book.*

fold something **over**† to double something over on itself; to make a fold in something. □ *I folded the paper over twice to make something I could fan myself with.*

fold something **up**† **1.** *Lit.* to double something over into its original folded position. □ *Please fold the paper up when you are finished.* **2.** *Fig.* to put an end to something; to close a money-losing enterprise. □ *Mr. Jones was going broke, so he folded his business up.*

fold up 1. *Lit.* [for something] to close by folding. □ *The table just folded up with no warning, trapping my leg.* **2.** *Fig.* [for someone] to faint. □ *She folded up when she heard the news.* **3.** *Fig.* [for a business] to cease operating. □ *Our shop finally folded up because of the recession.*

fool around to waste time doing something unnecessary or doing something amateurishly. □ *Stop fooling around and clean your room as I told you.*

force someone or something **down**† to press or push someone or something downward. □ *I forced him down and slipped the handcuffs on him.*

force something **down**† to force oneself to swallow something. □ *I can't stand sweet potatoes, but I manage to force them down just to keep from making a scene.*

force something **through** something to press or drive something through something that resists. □ *They forced the bill through the legislature.*

fork something **over**† **(to** someone**)** *Inf.* to give something to someone. (Usually refers to money.) □ *Come on! Fork the money over to me!*

freeze someone **out**† **1.** *Lit.* to make it too cold for some-one, usually by opening windows or through the use of air-conditioning. □ *Turn up the heat unless you're try-ing to freeze us out.* **2.** *Fig.* to lock someone out socially; to isolate someone from something or a group. □ *We didn't want to freeze you out. You failed to pay your dues, however.*

freshen up to get cleaned up, rested up, or restored. □ *I need a few minutes to freshen up before dinner.*

froth something **up**† to whip or aerate something until it is frothy. □ *Froth the milk up before you add it to the sauce.*

froth up [for something] to build up a froth when whipped, aerated, or boiled. □ *The mixture began to froth up as Dan beat it.*

fry something **up**† to cook something by frying. □ *Let's fry some chicken up for dinner.*

G

gasp something **out**† to utter something, gasping. □ Dan was just able to gasp out the instructions before he passed out.

gather something **in**† **1.** *Lit.* to collect something and bring it in; to harvest something. □ We gathered the pumpkins in just before Halloween. **2.** *Fig.* to fold or bunch cloth together when sewing or fitting clothing. □ Try gathering it in on each side to make it seem smaller.

gather something **up**† to collect something; to pick something up. □ Let's gather our things up and go.

gather together to assemble together. □ We will gather together on the main deck for a meeting.

get along **1.** [for people or animals] to be amiable with one another. □ Those two just don't get along. □ They seem to get along just fine. **2.** to leave; to be on one's way. □ I've got to get along. It's getting late.

get away to move away. (Often a command.) □ Get away! Don't bother me! □ I tried to get away, but he wouldn't let me.

get down **1.** *Sl.* to lay one's money on the table. (Gambling.) □ Okay, everybody get down. **2.** *Sl.* to concentrate; to do something well. □ I'm flunking two subjects, man. I gotta get down. □ Come on, Sam, pay attention. Get down and learn this stuff.

get out 1. [for someone or an animal] to depart to the outside or to escape. □ *When did your dog get out and run away?* **2.** [for information or a secret] to become publicly known. □ *We don't want the secret to get out.*

get someone **down** to depress a person; to make a person very sad. □ *My dog ran away, and it really got me down.*

get someone **up** to wake someone up; to get someone out of bed. □ *I've got to get John up, or he will be late for work.*

get something **down**† to manage to swallow something, especially something large or unpleasant. □ *The pill was huge, but I got it down.* □ *I get down all the pills despite their size.*

get something **out**† **1.** *Lit.* to remove or extricate something. □ *Please help me get this splinter out.* □ *Would you help me get out this splinter?* **2.** *Fig.* to manage to get something said. □ *He tried to say it before he died, but he couldn't get it out.*

get something **up**† to organize, plan, and assemble something. □ *Let's get a team up and enter the tournament.*

get up to wake up and get out of bed. □ *What time do you usually get up?* □ *I get up when I have to.*

give in cave in; to push in. □ *The rotting door gave in when we pushed, and we went inside.*

give out 1. to wear out and stop; to quit operating. □ *My old bicycle finally gave out.* □ *I think that your shoes are about ready to give out.* **2.** to be depleted. □ *The paper napkins gave out, and we had to use paper towels.* □ *The eggs gave out, and we had to eat cereal for breakfast for the rest of the camping trip.*

give someone or something **away**† to reveal a secret about someone or something. □ *I thought no one knew where I was, but my loud breathing gave me away.* □ *The cherry juice on his shirt gave him away.*

give someone or something **up**† **(for lost)** to abandon someone or something as being lost; to quit looking for someone or something that is lost. □ *After a week we had given the cat up for lost when suddenly she appeared.*

give someone or something **up**† **(to someone)** to hand someone or something over to someone; to relinquish claims on someone or something in favor of someone else. □ *We had to give the money we found up to the police.*

give something **off**† to release something, such as smoke, a noise, an odor, fragrance, etc. □ *The little animal gave a foul smell off.*

give something **out**† **1.** *Lit.* to distribute something; to pass something out. □ *The teacher gave the test papers out.* □ *The teacher gave out the papers.* **2.** *Fig.* to make something known to the public. □ *When will you give the announcement out?*

give something **up**† **1.** to forsake something; to stop using or eating something. □ *I gave coffee up because of the caffeine.* **2.** to quit doing something. □ *Oh, give it up! You're not getting anywhere.*

glass something **in**† to enclose something, such as a porch, in glass. □ *I want to glass this porch in, so we can use it in the winter.*

glue something **down**† to fix something down onto something with cement. □ *Glue the edge of the rug down before someone trips over it.*

glue something **together**† to attach the pieces of something together with glue. □ *She glued the pieces of the model plane together.*

go along 1. to continue; to progress. □ *Things are going along quite nicely in my new job.* □ *I hope everything is going along well.* **2.** to accompany [someone]. □ *Can I go along?*

go through to be approved; to succeed in getting through the approval process. □ *I sent the board of directors a proposal. I hope it goes through.*

go under 1. to sink beneath the surface of the water. □ *After capsizing, the ship went under very slowly.* □ *I was afraid that our canoe would go under in the rapidly moving water.* **2.** *Fig.* [for something] to fail. □ *The company went under exactly one year after it opened.* □ *We tried to keep it from going under.* **3.** *Fig.* to become unconscious from anesthesia. □ *After a few minutes, she went under and the surgeon began to work.*

gobble someone or something **up**† to eat someone or something completely and rapidly. □ *The wolf said that he was going to gobble the little girl up.*

gobble something **down**† to eat something very fast, swallowing large chunks. □ *The dog gobbled the meat down in seconds.*

gobble something **up**† to use up, buy up, or occupy all of something. □ *The shoppers gobbled all the sale merchandise up in a few hours.*

goof around to act silly. □ *The kids were all goofing around, waiting for the bus.*

goof off to waste time. □ *John is always goofing off.* □ *Quit goofing off and get to work!*

goof someone or something **up**† *Inf.* to mess someone or something up; to ruin someone's plans; to make something nonfunctional. □ *Who goofed this machine up?*

grind someone **down**† *Fig.* to wear someone down by constant requests; to wear someone down by constant nagging. □ *If you think you can grind me down by bothering me all the time, you are wrong.*

grind something **away**† to remove something by grinding. □ *Grind the bumps away and make the wall smooth.*

grind something **down**† to make something smooth or even by grinding. □ *Grind this down to make it smooth.*

grind something **up**† to pulverize or crush something by crushing, rubbing, or abrasion. □ *Please grind the fennel seeds up.*

gross someone **out**† to disgust someone. □ *Those horrible pictures just gross me out.* □ *Jim's story totally grossed out Sally.*

grow back [for something that has come off] to grow back again. (Includes parts of plants and some animals, fingernails, toenails, etc.) □ *The lizard's tail grew back in a few months.*

grow out [for something that has been cut back] to regrow. □ *Don't worry, your hair will grow out again.*

grow over something [for vegetation] to cover over something as it grows. □ *The vines grew over the shed and almost hid it from view.*

grow together [for things] to join together as they grow and develop. □ *Two of these trees grew together when they were much smaller.*

grow up to become mature; to become adult. □ *All the children have grown up and the parents are left with a lot of debts.*

guide something **away**† (**from** someone or something) **1.** to lead something away from someone or something. □ *I guided the lawn mower away from the children.* **2.** to channel or route something away from someone or something. □ *The farmer guided the creek water away from the main channel through a narrow ditch.*

gulp something **down**† to drink all of something, usually quickly. □ *He gulped his coffee down and left.*

gum something **up**† AND **gum the works up**† *Fig.* to make something inoperable; to ruin someone's plans. □ *Please, Bill, be careful and don't gum up the works.*

gun someone or an animal **down**† *Lit.* to shoot someone or an animal. □ *Max tried to gun a policeman down.*

guzzle something **down**† to drink something rapidly and eagerly. □ *He guzzled the beer down and called for another.*

H

hack something **down**† to chop something down. □ *Who hacked this cherry tree down?*

hack something **off**† to chop something off. □ *I need to get up that tree and hack that big branch off before it bangs on the house.*

hack something **up**† **1.** *Lit.* to chop something up into pieces. (Refers often to wood.) □ *Hack all this old furniture up, and we'll burn it in the fireplace.* **2.** *Fig.* to damage or mangle something. □ *Who hacked my windowsill up?*

ham something **up**† *Fig.* to make a performance seem silly by showing off or exaggerating one's part. (A show-off actor is known as a *ham*.) □ *Come on, Bob. Don't ham it up!*

hammer something **down**† to pound something down even with the surrounding surface. □ *Hammer all the nails down so that none of them will catch on someone's shoe.*

hammer something **home**† *Fig.* to try extremely hard to make someone understand or realize something. □ *The boss hopes to hammer the firm's poor financial position home to the staff.*

hammer something **out**† **1.** *Lit.* to hammer a dent away; to make a dent even with the surrounding surface. □

hammer something out (sense 3)

I'm going to have to have someone hammer this dent in my fender out. **2.** *Lit.* to expand something by hammering it thinner. □ *He hammered the gold out into a very thin sheet.* □ *He hammered out the gold into thin sheets.* **3.** *Fig.* to arrive at an agreement through argument and negotiation. □ *The two parties could not hammer a contract out.* **4.** *Fig.* to play something on the piano. □ *She hammered the song out loudly and without feeling.*

hand something **back**† **(to** someone**)** to return something to someone by hand. □ *Would you please hand this paper back to Scott?*

hand something **down**† **from** someone **to** someone to pass something down through many generations. □ *I hope we can make it a tradition to hand this down from generation to generation.*

hand something **down**† **(to** someone**). 1.** *Lit.* to pass something to a person on a lower level. □ *Hand this wrench* *down to the man under the sink.* **2.** *Fig.* to give something to a younger person. (Either at death or during life.) □ *John handed his old shirts down to his younger brother.* **3.** *Fig.* to announce or deliver a (legal) verdict or indictment. □ *The grand jury handed seven indictments down last week.*

hand something **in**[†] to submit something by hand. □ *Did you hand your application form in?*

hand something **off**[†] **(to** someone**) 1.** *Lit.* to give a football directly to another player. □ *Roger handed the ball off to Jeff.* □ *He handed off the ball.* **2.** *Fig.* to give something to someone else to do or complete. □ *I'm going to hand this assignment off to Jeff.*

hand something **out**[†] **(to** someone**) 1.** to give something out to someone. □ *The judge was known for handing heavy fines out.* **2.** to pass something, usually papers, out to people. □ *The teacher handed the tests out to the students.*

hand something **over** to give something (to someone); to relinquish something (to someone); to turn something over (to someone). □ *Come on, John! Hand over my wallet.*

hang on 1. to wait awhile. □ *Hang on a minute. I need to talk to you.* □ *Hang on. Let me catch up with you.* **2.** to survive for awhile. **3.** [for an illness] to linger or persist. □ *This cold has been hanging on for a month.* **4.** be prepared for fast or rough movement. (Usually a command.) □ *Hang on! The train is going very fast.* □ *Hang on! We're going to crash!* **5.** to pause in a telephone conversation. □ *Please hang on until I get a pen.*

hang out (some place**) 1.** to spend time in a place habitually. □ *Is this where you guys hang out all the time?*

2. to spend time aimlessly; to waste time. □ *Bill: What are you doing this afternoon? Tom: Oh, I'll just hang out.*

hang something **up**† to return the telephone receiver to its cradle. □ *Please hang this up when I pick up the other phone.* □ *Please hang up the phone.*

hang up 1. [for a machine or a computer] to grind to a halt; to stop because of some internal complication. □ *Our computer hung up right in the middle of printing the report.* □ *I was afraid that my computer would hang up permanently.* **2.** to replace the telephone receiver after a call; to terminate a telephone call. □ *I said good-bye and hung up.*

harness an animal **up**† to put a harness on an animal, such as a horse. □ *You had better harness the horses up so we can go.*

haul someone **in**† *Fig.* to arrest someone; [for a police officer] to take someone to the police station. □ *The cop hauled the drunk driver in.*

head back (some place**)** to start moving back to some place. □ *I walked to the end of the street and then headed back home.*

head someone or something **off**† *Fig.* to intercept and divert someone or something. □ *I think I can head her off before she reaches the police station.* □ *I hope we can head off trouble.*

head something **up**† **1.** *Lit.* to get something pointed in the right direction. (Especially a herd of cattle or a group of covered wagons.) □ *Head those wagons up—we're moving out.* **2.** *Fig.* to be in charge of something; to be the head of some organization. □ *I was asked to head the new committee up for the first year.*

heap something **up**† to make something into a pile. □ *He heaped the mashed potatoes up on my plate, because he thought I wanted lots.*

hear someone **out**† **1.** *Lit.* to hear all of what someone has to say. (Fixed order.) □ *Please hear me out. I have more to say.* □ *Hear out the witness. Don't jump to conclusions.* **2.** *Fig.* to hear someone's side of the story. (Fixed order.) □ *Let him talk! Hear him out! Listen to his side!*

heat something **up**† **(to** something**)** to raise the temperature of something to a certain level. □ *Please heat this room up to about seventy degrees.*

heat up 1. *Lit.* to get warmer or hot. □ *It really heats up in the afternoon around here.* □ *How soon will dinner be heated up?* **2.** *Fig.* to grow more animated or combative. □ *The debate began to heat up near the end.*

hedge someone **in**† *Fig.* to restrict someone. (See also **hedge** someone or something **in.**) □ *Our decision hedged in the children so they could not have any flexibility.*

hedge someone or something **in**† to enclose someone or something in a hedge. □ *Their overgrown yard has almost hedged us in.*

help someone **along 1.** to help someone move along. □ *I helped the old man along.* □ *Please help her along. She has a hurt leg.* **2.** to help someone advance. □ *I am more than pleased to help you along with your math.*

help (someone**) out**† to help someone do something; to help someone with a problem. □ *I am trying to raise this window. Can you help me out?*

help someone **up**† **(from** something**)** to help someone rise up from something; to help someone get up from something. □ *She offered to help him up from the chair.*

hem someone or something **in**† *Fig.* to trap or enclose someone or something. □ *The large city buildings hem me in.*

hew something **down**† to fell something wooden, usually a tree. □ *We will have to hew most of this forest down.*

hike something **up**† to raise something, such as prices, interest rates, a skirt, pants legs, etc. □ *The grocery store is always hiking prices up.*

hire someone or something **out**† to grant someone the use or efforts of someone or something for pay. □ *I hired my son out as a lawn-care specialist.*

hit someone **up**† **(for** something**)** to ask someone for a loan of money or for some other favor. □ *The tramp hit up each tourist for a dollar.*

hit something **off**† to begin something; to launch an event. □ *She hit off the fair with a speech.*

hold on to be patient. □ *Just hold on. Everything will work out in good time.* □ *If you will just hold on, everything will probably be all right.*

hold one's **end up**† to carry one's share of the burden; to do one's share of the work. □ *You're not holding your end up. We're having to do your share of the work.*

hold someone or something **off**† AND **keep** someone or something **off**† **1.** *Lit.* to do something physical to keep someone or something away; to stave someone or something off. □ *Tom was trying to rob us, but we managed to hold him off.* □ *I couldn't keep off the reporters any longer.* **2.** *Fig.* to make someone or something wait. □ *I know a lot of people are waiting to see me. Hold them off for a while longer.*

hold someone or something **over**† to retain someone or something (for a period of time). □ *The storm held John over for another day.*

hold someone or something **up**† **1.** *Lit.* to keep someone or something upright. □ *Johnny is falling asleep. Please hold him up until I prepare the bed for him.* **2.** *Fig.* to rob someone or a group. □ *Some punk tried to hold me up.* □ *The mild-looking man held up the bank and shot a teller.* **3.** *Fig.* to delay someone or something. □ *Driving the kids to school held me up.*

hold something **out**† **(to** someone**)** to offer something to someone. □ *I held a bouquet of roses out to her.*

hold up 1. *Lit.* to endure; to last a long time. □ *How long will this cloth hold up?* □ *I want my money back for this chair. It isn't holding up well.* **2.** AND **hold up (for** someone or something**)** to wait; to stop and wait for someone or something. □ *Hold up for Wallace. He's running hard to catch up to us.*

hollow something **out**† to make the inside of something hollow. □ *Martha hollowed the book out and put her money inside.*

hook something **down**† **1.** *Lit.* to attach something and hold it down with a hook. □ *Please hook the lid down so it doesn't fall off.* □ *Please hook down the lid.* **2.** *Sl.* to toss something down to someone. □ *Hook another can of beer down to me, will you?* **3.** *Sl.* to eat something quickly; to gobble something up. □ *Wally hooked the first hamburger down and ordered another.*

hook something **up**† to set something up and get it working. (The object is to be connected to a power supply, electronic network, telephone lines, etc.) □ *Will it take long to hook the telephone up?*

hop in(to something**)** to jump into something; to get into something. □ *Hop into your car and drive over to my house.* □ *I hopped in and drove off.*

hose someone or something **down**† to wash something down with water from a hose. □ *Hose her down to cool her off and maybe she will do the same for you.* □ *Please hose down the driveway.*

hound someone or an animal **down**† to pursue and capture someone or an animal. □ *I will hound the killer down if it takes me the rest of my life.*

hunch something **up**† to raise up or lift up some body part, usually the shoulders. □ *He hunched his shoulders up in his effort to get warm.*

hunch up to squeeze or pull the parts of one's body together. □ *Why is that child hunched up in the corner?*

hunker down (on something**)** *Fig.* to squat down on one's heels, a stool, a stone, etc. □ *Jeff hunkered down on the pavement and watched the world go by.*

hunt someone or something **down**† **1.** to chase and catch someone or something. □ *I don't know where Amy is, but I'll hunt her down. I'll find her.* □ *I will hunt down the villain.* **2.** to locate someone or something. □ *I don't have a big enough gasket. I'll have to hunt one down.*

hunt someone or something **out**† to find someone or something even if concealed. □ *We will hunt them all out and find every last one of those guys.* □ *We will hunt out all of them.*

hurl someone or something **down**† to throw or push someone or something downward to the ground. □ *Roger hurled the football down and it bounced away wildly.* □ *He hurled down the football in anger.*

hurl something **around**† to throw something, such as words, around carelessly. □ *Don't just go hurling foul words around like they didn't mean anything.* □ *You are just hurling around words!*

hurry someone or something **up** to make someone or something go or work faster. □ *Please hurry them all up. We are expecting to have dinner very soon.*

hush someone **up**† **1.** to make someone quiet. □ *Please hush the children up. I have a telephone call.* **2.** *Sl.* to kill someone. □ *The gang was afraid the witness would testify and wanted to hush him up.* □ *Mr. Big told Sam to hush up Richard.*

hush something **up**† *Fig.* to keep something a secret; to try to stop a rumor from spreading. □ *We wanted to hush up the story, but there was no way to do it.*

hush up to be quiet; to get quiet; to stop talking. □ *You talk too much. Hush up!*

I

ice something **down**† to cool something with ice. □ *They are icing the champagne down now.*

ice something **up**† to cause something to become icy. □ *I hope the cold doesn't ice the roads up.*

idle something **away**† *Fig.* to waste one's time in idleness; to waste a period of time, such as an afternoon, evening, one's life. □ *She idled the afternoon away and then went to a party.*

inch along (something) to move slowly along something little by little. □ *The cat inched along the carpet toward the mouse.*

ink something **in**† **1.** to fill in an outline with ink. □ *Please ink the drawing in with care.* **2.** to write something in ink. □ *Please ink your name in on the dotted line.*

intrude (up)on someone or something to encroach on someone or something or matters that concern only someone or something. (*Upon* is formal and less commonly used than *on*.) □ *I didn't mean to intrude upon you.* □ *Please don't intrude on our meeting. Please wait outside.*

inundate someone or something **with** something **1.** *Lit.* to flood someone or something with fluid. □ *The river inundated the fields with three feet of water.* □ *The storm inundated us with heavy rain.* **2.** *Fig.* to overwhelm someone with someone or something. □ *They inun-*

dated us with mail. □ *The children inundated us with requests for their favorite songs.* □ *The citizens inundated the legislature with demands for jobs.*

invite someone **out**[†] to ask someone out on a date. □ *I would love to invite you out sometime. If I did, would you go?*

invite someone **over**[†] **(for** something) to bid or request someone to come to one's house for something, such as a meal, party, chat, cards, etc. □ *Let's invite Tony and Nick over for dinner.*

iron something **out**[†] **1.** *Lit.* to use a flatiron to make cloth flat or smooth. □ *I will iron the drapes out, so they will hang together.* **2.** *Fig.* to ease a problem; to smooth out a problem. (Here *problem* is synonymous with *wrinkle.*) □ *It's only a little problem. I can iron it out very quickly.*

isolate someone or something **from** someone or something to keep people or things separated from one another, in any combination. □ *They isolated everyone from Sam, who was ill with malaria.* □ *We isolated the children from the source of the disease.*

itch for something *Fig.* to desire something. □ *I'm just itching for a visit from Amy.* □ *We are itching for some chocolate.*

J

jack something **up**† **1.** *Lit.* to raise something up on a mechanical lifting device. □ *Now I have to jack the car up, so I can change the tire.* □ *Please jack up the car.* **2.** *Fig.* to raise the price of something. □ *The store keeps jacking prices up.* □ *The grocery store jacked up the prices again last night.*

jam something **up**† **1.** to clog up something; to impede or block the movement of or through something. □ *Rachel jammed traffic up when her car stalled.* **2.** *Fig.* to force something upwards in haste or anger. □ *Who jammed the window up?*

jaw someone **down**† *Sl.* to talk someone down; to wear someone down talking. □ *We'll try to jaw him down. If that doesn't work, I don't know what we will do.*

jerk something **up**† **1.** to pull something up quickly. □ *He jerked his belt up tight.* **2.** to lift up something, such as ears, quickly. □ *The dog jerked its ears up.* □ *The dog jerked up its ears when it heard the floor creak.*

jostle someone **around**† to push or knock someone around. □ *Please don't jostle me around.*

jostle someone **aside**† to push or nudge someone aside. □ *Poor little Timmy was jostled aside by the crowd every time he got near the entrance.*

jot something **down**† to make a note of something. □ *This is important. Please jot this down.*

jumble something **up**† to make a hodgepodge out of things. □ *Who jumbled my papers up?*

K

keep off ((of) something) to remain off something; to stay off of something. (*Of* is usually retained before pronouns.) □ *Please keep off the grass.* □ *This is not a public thoroughfare! Keep off!*

keep on (doing something) to continue to do something. □ *Are you going to keep on singing all night?*

keep one's end up† **1.** *Lit.* to hold one's end of a load so that the load is level. □ *Be sure to keep your end up while we go up the stairs.* **2.** *Fig.* to carry through on one's part of a bargain. □ *You have to keep your end up like the rest of us.*

keep out (of something) **1.** *Lit.* to remain outside something or some place. □ *You should keep out of the darkroom when the door is closed.* **2.** *Fig.* to remain uninvolved with something. □ *Keep out of this! It's my affair.*

keep someone down to prevent someone from advancing or succeeding. □ *I don't think that this problem will keep her down.*

keep someone on *Fig.* to retain someone in employment longer than is required or was planned. □ *She worked out so well that we decided to keep her on.*

keep someone or something **back**† to hold someone or something in reserve. □ *We are keeping Karen back until the other players have exhausted themselves.*

keep someone or something **down** to hold someone or something in a hidden or protected position. □ *Please keep the noise down so Fred won't know it's a party when he comes in.*

keep someone **up 1.** *Lit.* to hold someone upright. □ *Try to keep him up until I can get his bed made.* **2.** *Fig.* to prevent someone from going to bed or going to sleep. □ *I'm sorry, was my trumpet keeping you up?*

keep something **down 1.** *Lit.* to make the level of noise lower and keep it lower. □ *Please keep it down. You are just too noisy.* **2.** *Fig.* to retain food in one's stomach rather than throwing it up. □ *I've got the flu and I can't keep any food down.* **3.** *Fig.* to keep spending under control. □ *I work hard to keep expenses down.*

keep something **up**† **1.** *Lit.* to hold or prop something up. □ *Keep your side of the trunk up. Don't let it sag.* **2.** *Fig.* to continue doing something. □ *I love your singing. Don't stop. Keep it up.* **3.** *Fig.* to maintain something in good order. □ *I'm glad you keep the exterior of your house up.*

kick back 1. *Inf.* to relax; to lean back and relax. □ *I really like to kick back and relax.* **2.** *Inf.* [for an addict] to return to an addiction or a habit, after having "kicked the habit." □ *Lefty kicked back after only a few days of being clean.*

kick one's **heels up**† *Fig.* to act frisky; to be lively and have fun. (Somewhat literal when said of hoofed animals.) □ *I like to go to an old-fashioned square dance and really kick up my heels.*

kick something around (sense 2)

kick someone or something **aside**† **1.** *Lit.* to get someone or something out of the way by kicking. □ *The bully kicked Timmy aside and grabbed our cake.* **2.** *Fig.* to get rid of someone or something. □ *He simply kicked aside his wife and took up with some young chick.*

kick someone or something **away**† to force someone or something away by kicking. □ *Fred kicked the intruder away from the gun he had dropped on the floor.* □ *Then he kicked away the gun.* □ *The kickboxer kicked the mugger away.*

kick something **around**† **1.** *Lit.* to move something around by kicking it, as in play. □ *Kick the ball around a while and then try to make a goal.* **2.** *Fig.* to discuss something; to chat about an idea. □ *We got together and kicked her idea around.*

kick something **down**† to break down something by kicking. □ *I was afraid they were going to kick the door down.*

kick something **in**† to break through something by kicking. □ *Tommy kicked the door in and broke the new lamp.* □ *He kicked in the door by accident.*

kick something **off**† *Fig.* to begin something; to hold a party or ceremony to mark the start of something. (Alludes to starting a football game by *kicking off* the ball for the first play.) □ *The city kicked the centennial celebration off with a parade.*

kick up to cause trouble or discomfort. □ *The ignition in my car is kicking up again. I will have to have it looked into.* □ *Aunt Jane's arthritis is kicking up. She needs to see the doctor again.*

kill someone or an animal **off**† to kill all of a group of people or creatures. □ *Lefty set out to kill Max and his boys off.*

kink up [for something] to develop kinks or tangles. □ *The leather parts tend to shrink and kink up in the damp weather.*

kiss someone or something **off**† *Fig.* to dismiss someone or something lightly; to abandon or write off someone or something. □ *I kissed off about $200 on that last deal.*

knit something **together**† to join things together by knitting. □ *Terry knitted the parts of the sweater together.*

knock someone or something **down**† to thrust someone or something to the ground by hitting. □ *The force of the blast knocked us down.*

knock someone or something **over**† to push or strike someone or something, causing the person or the thing to fall. □ *I am sorry. I didn't mean to knock you over. Are you hurt?* □ *Who knocked over this vase?*

knock someone **out**† **1.** *Lit.* to knock someone unconscious. (*Someone* includes *oneself.*) □ *Fred knocked Mike out and left him there in the gutter.* **2.** *Fig.* to make someone unconsciousness. □ *The drug knocked her out quickly.* □ *The powerful medicine knocked out the patient.* **3.** *Fig.* to surprise or please someone. □ *I have some news that will really knock you out.* **4.** *Fig.* to wear someone out; to exhaust someone. □ *All that exercise really knocked me out.*

knock someone **up**† *Inf.* to make a woman pregnant. □ *They say it was Willie who knocked her up.*

knock something **back**† *Sl.* to drink down a drink of something, especially something alcoholic. □ *I don't see how he can knock that stuff back.* □ *John knocked back two beers in ten minutes.*

knock something **off**† **1.** to manufacture or make something, especially in haste. □ *I'll see if I can knock another one off before lunch.* □ *They knocked off four window frames in an hour.* **2.** to knock off some amount from the price of something, lowering its price. □ *The store manager knocked 30 percent off the price of the coat.* □ *Can't you knock something off on this damaged item?* **3.** to copy or reproduce a product. □ *The manufacturer knocked off a famous designer's coat.* □ *They are well-known for knocking off cheap versions of expensive watches.*

knock something **out**† **1.** to create something hastily. □ *He knocked a few out as samples.* □ *He knocked out a few of them quickly, just so we could see what they were going to look like.* **2.** *Fig.* to put something out of order; to make something inoperable. □ *The storm knocked the telephone system out.*

knock something **over**† to tip something over. □ *Someone knocked the chair over.*

knock something **together**† to assemble something hastily. □ *I knocked this model together so you could get a general idea of what I had in mind.* □ *See if you can knock together a quick snack.*

knot something **together**† to tie something together in a knot. □ *Knot these strings together and trim the strings off the knot.* □ *Are the ropes knotted together properly?*

L

lace someone **up**† to tie someone's laces; to help someone get dressed in a garment having laces. □ *Would you please lace me up? I can't reach the ties in the back.*

lace something **up**† to tie the laces of something. □ *Lace your shoes up, Tommy.*

ladle something **up**† to scoop something up in a ladle. □ *Jerry ladled a cool dipper of water up and quenched his thirst.*

lap something **up**† **1.** *Lit.* [for an animal] to lick something up. □ *The dog lapped the ice cream up off the floor.* **2.** *Fig.* [for someone] to accept or believe something with enthusiasm. □ *Of course, they believed it. They just lapped it up.*

lash someone or something **down**† to tie someone or something down. □ *The villain lashed Nell down to the railroad tracks.* □ *He lashed down the innocent victim.*

lash something **about** to whip or fling something about violently. □ *The big cat lashed its tail threateningly.*

last out to hold out; to endure. □ *How long can you last out? I don't think we can last out much longer without food and water.*

last something **out**† to endure until the end of something. □ *Ed said that he didn't think he could last the opera out and left.*

lather up 1. [for a horse] to develop a foam of sweat from working very hard. □ *The horses lathered up heavily during the race.* **2.** [for soap] to develop thick suds when rubbed in water. □ *This soap won't lather up, even when I rub it hard.* **3.** AND **lather** oneself **up** [for one] to apply soap lather to one's body. □ *He will spend a few minutes lathering himself up before he rinses.* □ *He lathered up and then shaved.*

laugh something **away**† **1.** to spend an amount of time laughing. □ *We laughed the hour away listening to the comedian.* **2.** to get rid of something negative by laughing. □ *Kelly knows how to laugh her problems away, and it cheers up the rest of us too.*

laugh something **off**† to treat a serious problem lightly by laughing at it. □ *Although his feelings were hurt, he just laughed the incident off as if nothing had happened.*

lay someone **away**† *Euph.* to bury someone. □ *Yes, he has passed. We laid him away last week.*

lay someone **out**† **1.** *Sl.* to knock someone down with a punch; to knock someone unconscious. □ *Tom laid out Bill with one punch to the chin.* **2.** to prepare a corpse for burial or for a wake. □ *They laid out their uncle for the wake.* **3.** *Sl.* to scold someone severely. □ *Don't lay me out! I didn't do it!* □ *She really laid out the guy but good. What did he do, rob a bank?*

lay someone **up**† to cause someone to be ill in bed. □ *A broken leg laid me up for two months.*

lay something **aside**† to set something aside; to place something to one side, out of the way. □ *He laid his papers aside and went out to welcome the visitor.*

lay something **in**† to get something and store it for future use. □ *They laid a lot of food in for the holidays.*

lay something **out**† **1.** *Lit.* to spread something out. □ *The nurse laid the instruments out for the operation.* **2.** *Fig.* to explain a plan of action or a sequence of events. □ *Let me lay it out for you.* □ *Lay out the plan very carefully, and don't skip anything.* **3.** *Fig.* to spend some amount of money. □ *I can't lay that kind of money out every day!*

lay something **up**† **1.** to acquire and store something. □ *Try to lay as much of it up as you can.* □ *I am trying to lay up some firewood for the winter.* **2.** [for something] to disable something. □ *The accident laid up the ship for repairs.*

lead off to be the first one to go or leave. □ *You lead off. I'll follow.* □ *Mary led off and the others followed closely behind.*

lead someone **on 1.** to guide someone onward. □ *We led him on so he could see more of the gardens.* **2.** AND **lead** someone **on**† to tease someone; to encourage someone's romantic or sexual interest without sincerity. □ *You are just leading me on!* □ *It's not fair to continue leading him on.*

lead on to continue to lead onward. □ *The guide led on and we followed.* □ *Lead on, my friend. We are right behind you!*

lead someone or something **off**† to guide someone or something away. □ *The guide led the hikers off on the adventure of their lives.*

leak out [for information] to become known unofficially. □ *I hope that news of the new building does not leak out before the contract is signed.*

lean over 1. to bend over. □ *Lean over and pick the pencil up yourself! I'm not your servant!* □ *As Kelly leaned* *over to tie her shoes, her chair slipped out from under her.* **2.** to tilt over. □ *The fence leaned over and almost fell.*

leave something **aside**† **1.** to leave something in reserve. □ *Leave some of the sugar aside for use in the icing.* **2.** to ignore something, especially a fact. □ *Let's leave the question of who will pay for it aside for a while.* □ *We will leave aside the current situation and talk about the future.*

leave something **on**† **1.** to continue to wear some article of clothing. □ *I think I will leave my coat on. It's chilly in here.* **2.** to allow something [that can be turned off] to remain on. □ *Who left the radio on?*

lend something **out**† **(to** someone**)** to allow someone to borrow something. □ *I lent my tuxedo out to a friend who was going to a dance, and now I haven't anything to wear to the opera.* □ *I lent out my copy of the book.*

let someone **down** to disappoint someone; to fail someone. □ *I'm sorry I let you down. Something came up, and I couldn't meet you.*

let someone **off**† to permit someone to disembark or leave a means of transportation. □ *The driver let Mary off the bus.* □ *"I can't let you off at this corner," said the driver.*

let something **out**† **1.** *Fig.* to reveal something; to tell about a secret or a plan. □ *It was supposed to be a secret. Who let it out?* □ *Who let out the secret?* **2.** *Fig.* to enlarge an article of clothing. □ *She had to let her overcoat out because she had gained some weight.*

level off [for variation or fluctuation in the motion of something] to diminish; [for a rate] to stop increasing or decreasing. □ *The plane leveled off at 10,000 feet.* □ *After a while the workload will level off.*

level out [for something that was going up and down] to assume a more level course or path. □ *The road leveled out after a while and driving was easier.*

level something **down** to make something level or smooth. □ *The soil is very uneven in this part of the garden. Would you please level it down?* □ *The huge earth-moving machines leveled the hill down in preparation for the building of the highway.*

level something **off**† to make something level or smooth. □ *You are going to have to level the floor off before you put the carpet down.*

level something **out**† to cause something to assume a more level course or path. □ *Level this path out before you open it to the public.*

level something **up**† to move something into a level or plumb position. □ *Use a piece of wood under the table's leg to level it up.*

lift someone or something **up**† to raise someone or something. □ *I helped lift him up and put him on the stretcher.*

lift something **off (of)** someone or something AND **lift** something **off**† to raise something and uncover or release someone or something. (*Of* is usually retained before pronouns.) □ *Lift the beam off of him and see if he is still breathing.*

lift up to raise up. □ *Suddenly, the top of the box lifted up and a hand reached out.* □ *Bill's hand lifted up and fell back again.*

light something **up**† **1.** to light a fire, a gas burner, etc. □ *I lit the kindling up and soon the fire was going.* **2.** to light something to smoke, such as a cigarette, pipe, etc.

113

□ *She lit the cigarette up and took in a great breath of the smoke.*

light up 1. to become brighter. □ *Suddenly, the sky lit up like day.* □ *The room lit up as the fire suddenly came back to life.* **2.** [for someone] to become interested and responsive in something. □ *We could tell from the way Sally lit up that she recognized the man in the picture.*

lighten something **up**† to make something lighter or brighter. □ *Some white paint will lighten this room up a lot.*

limber someone or something **up**† to make someone or something more flexible or loose. □ *Let me give you a massage; that will limber you up.*

line someone or something **up**† **1.** *Lit.* to put people or things in line. □ *Line everyone up and march them onstage.* □ *Line up the kids, please.* □ *Please line these books up.* **2.** *Fig.* to schedule someone or something [for something]. □ *Please line somebody up for the entertainment.* □ *We will try to line up a magician and a clown for the party.*

linger on to remain for a long time; to exist longer than would have been thought. □ *This cold of mine just keeps lingering on.*

liquor someone **up**† to get someone tipsy or drunk. □ *He liquored her up and tried to take her home with him.*

liquor up to drink an alcoholic beverage, especially to excess. □ *Sam sat around all evening liquoring up.*

litter something **up**† to mess something up with litter, trash, possessions, etc. □ *Who littered this room up?*

live something **down**† to overcome the shame or embarrassment of something. □ *You'll live it down someday.*

live something **out**† to act out something such as one's fantasies. □ *She tried to live her dreams out.*

live something **over** to go back and live a part of one's life again in order to do things differently. □ *I wish I could go back and live those days over again. Boy, would I do things differently!*

live together 1. [for two people] to dwell in the same place. □ *I live together with my sister in the house my parents left us.* **2.** [for two people] to dwell together in a romantic relationship. □ *I heard that Sally and Sam are living together.*

liven something **up**† to make something more lively or less dull. □ *Some singing might liven things up a bit.*

loaf around to waste time; to idle the time away doing almost nothing. □ *Every time I see you, you are just loafing around.*

lock someone or something **up**† **(somewhere)** to lock someone or something within something or some place. □ *The captain ordered the sailor locked up in the brig until the ship got into port.* □ *Don't lock me up!*

lock something **in**† to make something, such as a rate of interest, permanent over a period of time. □ *You should try to lock in a high percentage rate on your bonds.*

log off AND **log out** to record one's exit from a computer system. (This action may be recorded, or logged, automatically in the computer's memory.) □ *I closed my files and logged off.*

log on to begin to use a computer system, as by entering a password, etc. (This action may be recorded, or logged, automatically in the computer's memory.) □ *What time did you log on to the system this morning?*

loll around to roll, flop, or hang around. □ *The dog's tongue lolled around as it rolled on its back, trying to keep cool.*

look on to be a spectator and watch what is happening without participating. □ *The beating took place while a policeman looked on.*

loom up to appear to rise up [from somewhere]; to take form or definition, usually threatening to some degree. □ *A great city loomed up in the distance. It looked threatening in the dusky light.* □ *A ghost loomed up, but we paid no attention, since it had to be a joke.*

loosen up to become loose or relaxed. □ *We tried to get Mary to loosen up, but she did not respond.*

loosen someone **up**† *Fig.* to make someone or a group more relaxed and friendly. □ *I loosened up the audience with a joke.*

lope along to move along, bounding. □ *The dog loped along at an even pace, answering to his master's whistle.*

luck out to be fortunate; to strike it lucky. □ *I didn't luck out at all. I rarely make the right choice.*

lumber along to lope or walk along heavily and awkwardly. □ *The horses were lumbering along very slowly because they were tired out.*

lumber off to move or lope away heavily and awkwardly. □ *The frightened bear lumbered off, and we left in a hurry.*

lurch forward to jerk or sway forward. □ *When the train lurched forward, we were pushed back into our seats.*

lurk around to slink or sneak around somewhere. □ *Who is that guy lurking around the building?*

M

make one's **mind up**† **(about** someone or something**)** to decide about someone or something. □ *Please make your mind up about Ralph. Will you pick him or not?* □ *Make up your mind about her!*

make someone's **mind up**† to decide; to do something that decides something for someone. □ *Will you please make up your mind?*

make someone **up**† to put makeup on someone. □ *You have to make the clowns up before you start on the other characters in the play.*

make something **out**† to see, read, or hear something well enough to understand it. □ *What did you say? I couldn't quite make it out.*

make something **up**† **1.** to redo something; to do something that one has failed to do in the past. □ *Can I make the lost time up?* □ *Can I make up the test that I missed?* **2.** to assemble something. □ *We will ship the parts to China where we will make up the computers with cheap labor.* □ *Have they finished making up the pages for the next edition of the magazine?* **3.** to think up something; to make and tell a lie. □ *That's not true! You just made that up!* □ *I didn't make it up!* **4.** to mix something up; to assemble something. □ *John: Is my prescription ready? Druggist: No, I haven't made it up yet.*

map something out

make something **up**† **from** something to create something from something. □ *I will make some stew up from the ingredients available in the fridge.*

map something **out**† to plot something out carefully, usually on paper. □ *I have a good plan. I will map it out for you.*

mar something **up**† to dent or scratch something; to harm the smooth finish of something. □ *Please don't mar the furniture up.*

mark someone **down**† [for a teacher] to give someone a low score. □ *He'll mark you down for misspelled words.* □ *I marked down Tom for bad spelling.*

mark someone or something **off**† AND **mark** someone or something **out**† to cross off the name of someone or something. □ *They were late, so I marked them off.* □ *I marked off the late people.*

mark something **down**† **1.** *Lit.* to write something down on paper. □ *She marked the number down on the paper.*

2. *Fig.* to reduce the price of something. □ *We are going to mark all this merchandise down next Monday.*

mark something **up**† **1.** to mess something up with marks. □ *Don't mark up your book!* □ *Who marked this book up?* **2.** to grade a paper and make lots of informative marks and comments on it. □ *The teacher really marked up my term paper.* **3.** to raise the price of something. □ *The grocery store seems to mark the price of food up every week.*

marry someone **off**† **(to** someone**)** to manage to get someone married to someone and out of the house or family. □ *Her parents wanted nothing more than to marry her off to a doctor.*

mash something **up**† to crush something into a paste or pieces. □ *Mash the potatoes up and put them in a bowl.*

mask something **out**† to conceal or cover part of something from view. □ *The trees masked the city dump out, so it could not be seen from the street.*

match up [for things or people] to match, be equal, or complementary. □ *These match up. See how they are the same length?*

max out to reach one's maximum in something, such as weight in weight lifting or credit on a credit card. □ *Andy finally maxed out at 300 pounds.*

measure something **off**† to determine the length of something. □ *He measured the length of the room off and wrote down the figure in his notebook.* □ *Fred measured off the width of the house.*

measure something **out**† to measure and distribute something as it is being taken out, unwrapped, unfolded, etc. □ *Carl measured the grain out a cup at a time.*

mellow out 1. to become less angry. □ *When you mellow out, maybe we can talk.* □ *Come on, man, stop yelling and mellow out!* **2.** to become generally more relaxed. □ *Gary was nearly forty before he started to mellow out a little and take life less seriously.*

melt away to melt into a liquid. □ *When the wax candles melted away, they ruined the lace tablecloth.*

melt down 1. *Lit.* [for something frozen] to melt. □ *The glacier melted down little by little.* □ *When the ice on the streets melted down, it was safe to drive again.* **2.** *Fig.* [for a nuclear reactor] to become hot enough to melt through its container.

melt something **away**† to cause something to melt into a liquid. □ *The sun melted the ice away.*

melt something **down**† to cause something frozen to melt; to cause something solid to melt. □ *The rays of the sun melted the candle down to a puddle of wax.*

mess around AND **mess about 1.** to waste time; to do something ineffectually. □ *Stop messing around and get busy.* □ *I wish you wouldn't mess about so much. You waste a lot of time that way.* **2.** to play [with someone] sexually. □ *Pete was messing around with Maria during the summer.*

mess up to make an error; to do something wrong; to flub up. □ *I hope I don't mess up on the quiz.*

mess something **up**† to make something disorderly; to create disorder in something; to throw someone's plans awry. □ *You really messed this place up!*

mete something **out**† to measure something out. □ *She meted the solution out carefully into a row of test tubes.*

mix in (with someone or something**)** to mix or combine with people or substances. □ *The band came down from the stage and mixed in with the guests during the break.*

mix someone **up**† to confuse someone. □ *Please don't ask questions now; you'll mix me up!*

mix something **up**† to bring something into disorder; to throw something into a state of confusion. □ *Don't mix up the papers on my desk.*

mock something **up**† to make a model or simulation of something. □ *The engineers mocked the new car design up for the managers to see.*

mop something **down**† to clean a surface with a mop. □ *Please mop this floor down now.*

mop something **off**† to wipe the liquid off something. □ *Please mop the counter off with paper towels.*

mop something **up**† to clean up something, such as a spill, with a mop or with a mopping motion. □ *Please mop this mess up.*

motion someone **aside**† to give a hand signal to someone to move aside. □ *He motioned her aside and had a word with her.* □ *I motioned aside the guard and asked him a question.*

mound something **up**† to form something into a mound. □ *Please mound up the leaves around the rosebushes.*

mount up 1. to get up on a horse. □ *Mount up and let's get out of here!* **2.** [for something] to increase in amount or extent. □ *Expenses really mount up when you travel.*

mouth off to speak out of turn; to backtalk. □ *If you mouth off, I will ground you for three weeks.*

move along to continue to move; to start moving out of the way. (Often a command.) □ *The crowd moved along slowly.*

move on to continue moving; to travel on; to move along and not stop or tarry. □ *Move on! Don't stop here!*

move out (of some place) **1.** to leave a place; to leave; to begin to depart. (Especially in reference to a large number of persons or things.) □ *The crowd started to move out of the area about midnight.* **2.** to leave a place of residence permanently. □ *We didn't like the neighborhood, so we moved out of it.*

move over to move a bit [away from the speaker]. □ *Move over. I need some space.* □ *Please move over. Part of this space is mine.*

move someone or something **forward** to cause someone or something to advance. □ *Move her forward. She is too far back.*

move someone **up**† to advance or promote someone. □ *We are ready to move you up. You have been doing quite well.*

move up to advance; to go higher. □ *Isn't it about time that I move up? I've been an office clerk for over a year.*

muddle something **up**† to mix something up; to make something confusing. □ *You really muddled the language of this contract up.*

mull something **over**† to think about something; to ponder or worry about something. □ *That's an interesting idea, but I'll have to mull it over.*

muss someone or something **up**† to put someone or something into disarray. □ *Don't muss me up!* □ *You mussed up my hair.*

N

nail someone **down**† **(on** something**)** Go to pin someone down† **(on** something**)**.

nail something **down**† to secure something down by nailing it. □ *Please nail the floorboard down or someone will trip over it.* □ *I'll nail down these floorboards.*

nail something **up**† **1.** to put something up, as on a wall, by nailing. □ *Please nail this up.* □ *I'll nail up this picture for you.* **2.** to nail something closed; to use nails to secure something from intruders. □ *Sam nailed the door up so no one could use it.*

nick something **up**† to make little dents or nicks in something, ruining the finish. □ *Someone nicked the kitchen counter up.*

nudge someone or something **aside**† to push or bump someone or something out of the way. □ *We nudged the old man aside and went on ahead.*

nurse someone or an animal **along**† to aid or encourage the well-being or return to health of someone or an animal. □ *She nursed the old man along for a few years until he died.* □ *She nursed along the invalid.*

O

offer something **up**† **(to** someone or something) to give something to someone or something as a mark of devotion, thanks, etc. □ *We offered up our gratitude to the queen.*

open someone **up**† *Fig.* to perform a surgical operation requiring a major incision on someone. □ *The doctor had to open George up to find out what was wrong.*

open something **out**† to unfold or expand something; to open and spread something out. □ *When she opened the fan out, she saw it was made of plastic.*

open something **up**† **1.** *Lit.* to unwrap something; to open something. □ *Yes, I want to open my presents up.* □ *I can't wait to open up my presents.* **2.** *Fig.* to begin examining or discussing something. □ *Do you really want to open it up now?* □ *Now is the time to open up the question of taxes.* **3.** *Fig.* to reveal the possibilities of something; to reveal an opportunity. □ *Your letter opened new possibilities up.* **4.** *Fig.* to start the use of something, such as land, a building, a business, etc. □ *They opened the coastal lands up to resort development.* □ *We opened up a new store last March.* **5.** *Fig.* to make a vehicle go as fast as possible. (As in opening up the throttle.) □ *We took the new car out on the highway and opened it up.* **6.** to make something less congested. □ *They opened the yard up by cutting out a lot of old shrubbery.*

open up 1. *Lit.* open your door; open your mouth. (Usually **Open up!**) □ *I want in. Open up!* □ *Open up! This is the police.* **2.** *Fig.* to become available. □ *A new job is opening up at my office.* **3.** *Fig.* to go as fast as possible. (As in opening up the throttle.) □ *I can't get this car to open up. Must be something wrong with the engine.* **4.** to become clear, uncluttered, or open. □ *The sky opened up, and the sun shone.*

order something **in**† to have something, usually food, brought into one's house or place of business. □ *Do you want to order pizza in?*

P

pace around AND **pace about** to walk around nervously or anxiously. □ *Stop pacing around and sit down.* □ *There is no need to pace about.*

pace something **off**† to mark off a distance by counting the number of even strides taken while walking. □ *The farmer paced a few yards off and pounded a stake into the soil.*

pace something **out**† **1.** *Lit.* to measure a distance by counting the number of even strides taken while walking. □ *He paced the distance out and wrote it down.* **2.** *Fig.* to deal with a problem by pacing around. □ *When she was upset, she walked and walked while she thought through her problem. When Ed came into the room, she was pacing a new crisis out.*

pack down [for something] to settle down in a container. □ *The cereal has packed down in the box so that it seems that the box is only half full.*

pack someone **off**† **(to** someone or something) to send someone away to someone or some place. □ *Laura just packed all the kids off to summer camp.* □ *She packed off the kids to their camp.*

pack someone or something **together**† to press or squeeze people or things together. □ *The ushers packed the people together as much as they dared.* □ *They packed together all the people standing in the room.*

pare something down (to something)

pack something **away**† to pack something up and put it away. □ *Pack this mirror away where it will be safe.*

pack something **down**† to make something more compact; to press something in a container down so it takes less space. □ *The traffic packed down the snow.*

pack up to prepare one's belongings to be transported by placing them into a container; to gather one's things together for one's departure. □ *If we are going to leave in the morning, we should pack up now.* □ *I think you should pack up and be ready to leave at a moment's notice.*

pad something **out**† *Fig.* to make something appear to be larger or longer by adding unnecessary material. □ *If we pad the costume out here, it will make the person who wears it look much plumper.*

paint something **out**† to cover something up or obliterate something by applying a layer of paint. □ *The worker painted the graffiti out.*

pair off [for two people or other creatures] to form a couple or pair. □ *Everyone should pair off and discuss the issue for a while.*

pant something **out**† to tell something while panting for breath. □ *Laura had been running but she was able to pant the name of the injured person out.*

parcel something **up**† to wrap something up in a package. □ *Parcel up the files and place them on top of the file cabinet.*

pare something **down**† **(to something)** to cut someone down to something or a smaller size. □ *I will have to pare the budget down to the minimum.* □ *I hope we can pare down the budget.*

pass out to faint; to lose consciousness. □ *When he got the news, he passed out.*

pass someone or something **by**† to miss someone or something; to overlook someone or something. □ *The storm passed by the town leaving it unharmed.*

pass someone or something **up**† **1.** to fail to select someone or something. □ *The committee passed Jill up and chose Kelly.* □ *They passed up Jill.* **2.** to travel past someone or something. □ *We had to pass the museum up, thinking we could visit the next time we were in town.*

pass something **on**† **1.** *Lit.* to hand or give something (to another person). □ *Please pass on this book to the next person on the list.* **2.** *Fig.* to tell someone something; to spread news or gossip. □ *Don't pass this on, but Bill isn't living at home any more.*

paste something **up**† **1.** to repair something with paste. □ *See if you can paste this book up so it will hold together.* □ *Paste up the book and hope it holds together for a while.* **2.** to assemble a complicated page of material by pasting the parts together. □ *There is no way a typesetter can get this page just the way you want it. You'll have to paste it up yourself.*

pat something **down**† to tap something down with the open hand. □ *I heaped some soil over the seeds and patted it down.*

patch someone **up**† to give medical care to someone. □ *That cut looks bad, but the doc over there can patch you up.*

patch something **up**† **1.** *Lit.* to repair something in a hurry; to make something temporarily serviceable again. □ *Can you patch this up so I can use it again?* □ *I'll patch up the hose for you.* **2.** *Fig.* to "repair" the damage done by an argument or disagreement. □ *Mr. and Mrs. Smith are trying to patch things up.*

pay someone **back**† **1.** *Lit.* to return money that was borrowed from a person. □ *You owe me money. When are you going to pay me back?* □ *You must pay John back. You have owed him money for a long time.* **2.** *Fig.* to get even with someone [for doing something]. □ *I will pay her back for what she said about me.* □ *Fred eventually will pay Mike back. He bears grudges for a long time.*

pay someone **off**† **1.** *Lit.* to pay what is owed to a person. □ *I can't pay you off until Wednesday when I get my paycheck.* **2.** *Fig.* to bribe someone. □ *Max asked Lefty if he had paid the cops off yet.*

pay something **down**† **1.** *Lit.* to make a deposit of money on a purchase. □ *You will have to pay a lot of money down on a car that expensive.* **2.** *Fig.* to reduce a bill by paying part of it, usually periodically. □ *I think I can pay the balance down by half in a few months.*

pay something **off**† to pay all of a debt; to pay the final payment for something bought on credit. □ *This month I'll pay the car off.*

pay something **out**† to unravel or unwind wire or rope as it is needed. (See also **play** something **out**.) □ *One worker paid the cable out, and another worker guided it into the conduit.*

pay something **up**† to pay all of whatever is due; to complete all the payments on something. □ *Would you pay up your bills, please?*

pay up to pay what is owed. (Often a command: **Pay up!**) □ *I want my money now. Pay up!*

peal out [for bells or voices] to sound forth musically. □ *The bells pealed out to announce that the wedding had taken place.*

peel something **off**† **((of)** something**)** AND **peel** something **off**† **from** something to remove the outside surface layer from something. (*Of* is usually retained before pronouns.) □ *She carefully peeled the skin off the apple.*

pep someone or something **up**† to make someone or something more vigorous. □ *Nancy needs to take some vitamins to pep her up.* □ *The coffee break pepped up the tired workers.*

perk someone **up**† to make someone more cheery or refreshed. □ *A nice cup of coffee would really perk me up.*

perk something **up**† to refresh or brighten something; to make something more lively. □ *A bit of bright yellow here and there will perk this room up a lot.*

perk up to become invigorated; to become more active. □ *After a bit of water, the plants perked up nicely.*

peter out [for something] to die or dwindle away; [for something] to become exhausted gradually. □ *When the fire petered out, I went to bed.*

phone someone **up**† to call someone on the telephone. □ *I don't know what he will do. I will phone him up and ask him.*

pick someone or something **apart**† **1.** *Lit.* to pick at and pull someone or something to pieces. □ *The vultures attacked the hunger-weakened man and tried to pick him apart.* □ *They tried to pick apart the body.* **2.** *Fig.* to analyze and criticize someone or something negatively. □ *You didn't review her performance; you just picked her apart.*

pick someone up (sense 1)

pick someone or something **off**† *Fig.* to kill someone or something with a carefully aimed gunshot. □ *The hunter picked the deer off with great skill.* □ *The killer tried to pick off the police officer.*

pick someone or something **out**† **(for** someone or something**)** to choose someone or something to serve as someone or something. □ *I picked one of the new people out for Santa Claus this year.*

pick someone **up**† **1.** to attempt to become acquainted with someone for romantic or sexual purposes. □ *Who are you anyway? Are you trying to pick me up?* **2.** [for the police] to find and bring someone to the police station for questioning or arrest. □ *The cop tried to pick her up, but she heard him coming and got away.* □ *Sergeant Jones, go pick up Sally Franklin and bring her in to be questioned about the jewel robbery.* **3.** to stop one's car, bus, etc., and offer someone a ride. □ *Don't ever pick a stranger up when you're out driving!* **4.** to go to a place in a car, bus, etc., and take on a person as a passenger. □ *Please come to my office and pick me up at noon.*

pick something **over**† *Fig.* to look through something carefully, looking for something special. □ *The shoppers who got here first picked everything over, and there is not much left.*

pick something **up**† **1.** *Lit.* to lift up or raise something from a lower place. □ *Please help me pick this stuff up off the pavement.* **2.** *Fig.* to tidy up or clean up a room or some other place. □ *Let's pick this room up in a hurry.* □ *I want you to pick up the entire house.* **3.** *Fig.* to find, purchase, or acquire something. □ *Where did you pick that up?* □ *I picked up this tool at the hardware store.* **4.** *Fig.* to learn something. □ *I picked up a lot of knowledge about music from my brother.* **5.** *Fig.* to cause something to go faster, especially music. □ *All right, let's pick up the tempo and get it moving faster.* □ *Okay, get moving. Pick it up!* **6.** *Fig.* to resume something. □ *I'll have to pick up my work where I left off.* **7.** *Fig.* to receive radio signals; to bring something into view. □ *I can just pick it up with a powerful telescope.* □ *I can hardly pick up a signal.* **8.** *Fig.* to find a trail or route. □ *You should pick up Highway 80 in a few miles.*

piddle something **away**† *Fig.* to waste away money or a period of time. □ *Please don't piddle all your money away.*

piece something **out**† **1.** *Lit.* to add patches or pieces to something to make it complete. □ *There is not quite enough cloth to make a shirt, but I think I can piece it out with some scraps of a complementary color for the collar.* **2.** *Fig.* to add missing parts to a story, explanation, or narrative to make it make sense. □ *Before she passed out, she muttered a few things and we were able to piece the whole story out from that.*

pile something **up**† **1.** to crash or wreck something. □ *Drive carefully if you don't want to pile the car up.* □ *The driver piled up the car against a tree.* **2.** to make something into a heap. □ *Carl piled all the leaves up and set them afire.*

pile up 1. *Lit.* [for things] to gather or accumulate. □ *The newspapers began to pile up after a few days.* **2.** *Fig.* [for a number of vehicles] to crash together. □ *Nearly twenty cars piled up on the bridge this morning.*

pin someone **down**† **(on** something) AND **nail** someone **down**† **(on** something) *Fig.* to demand and receive a firm answer from someone to some question. (Alludes to shifting from answer to answer; commit to one answer or another.) □ *I tried to pin him down on a time and place, but he was very evasive.* □ *Don't try to pin down the mayor on anything!*

pin something **back**† to hold something back by pinning. □ *I will pin the curtains back to let a little more light in.* □ *Jane pinned back the curtains.*

pin something **down**† AND **nail** something **down**† **1.** *Lit.* to attach or affix something with nails or pins. □ *Pin the pattern down temporarily.* □ *Nail down this piece of flooring every 12 inches.* **2.** *Fig.* to determine or fix something, such as a date, an agreement, an amount of money, a decision, etc. □ *It will be ready sometime next month. I can't pin the date down just yet, however.*

pinch something **back**† to pinch off a bit of the top of a plant so it will branch and grow more fully. □ *You should pinch this back so it will branch.*

pinch something **off (of)** something AND **pinch** something **off**† to sever something from something by pinching. (*Of* is usually retained before pronouns.) □ *Pinch the* *buds off the lower branches so the one at the top will bloom.*

pipe down to become quiet; to cease making noise; to shut up. (Especially as a rude command.) □ *Pipe down! I'm trying to sleep.*

pitch forward to jerk or thrust forward. □ *Suddenly the car pitched forward, jerking the passengers around.* □ *We pitched forward inside the car as we went over the bumpy road.*

pitch something **away**† to toss or throw something away. □ *He pitched the broken stick away, and looked around for something stronger.*

place something **aside**† to set something aside or out of the way. □ *Place this one aside and we'll keep it for ourselves.*

place something **down**† **(on** something**)** to put something down on something. □ *Place the book down on the top of the table.*

plan something **out**† to make thorough plans for something. □ *We sat down and planned out our strategy.*

plane something **away**† to smooth off bumps or irregularities with a plane. □ *Please plane the bumps away so that the board is perfectly smooth.*

plane something **down**† to smooth something down with a plane; to remove some material from something with a plane. □ *I planed down the edge of the door for you.*

plane something **off**† to remove bumps, nicks, or scrapes by planing. □ *Sam planed off the bumps.*

plaster something **up**† to close something up with plaster; to cover over holes or cracks in a wall with plaster. □ *You have to plaster up the cracks.*

play someone or something **down**† to lessen the effect or importance of someone or something. □ *John is a famous actor, but the director tried to play him down as just another member of the cast.*

play someone or something **up**† to make someone or something seem to be more important. □ *The director tried to play Ann up, but she was not really a star.*

play something **off**† to play a game to break a tied score. □ *They decided not to play the tie off because it had grown so late.*

play something **out**† **1.** to play something, such as a game, to the very end. □ *I was bored with the game, but I felt I had to play it out.* **2.** to unwind, unfold, or unreel something. (See also **pay** something **out**.) □ *Please play some more rope out.*

play something **over** to replay something, such as a game, a videotape, an audio recording, etc. □ *There was an objection to the way the referee handled the game, so they played it over.*

play something **through**† to play something, such as a piece of recorded music, all the way through. □ *I played the album through, hoping to find even one song I liked.*

play something **up**† to emphasize something; to be a booster of something. □ *The press played the scandal up so much that everyone became bored with it.*

play through [for golfers] to pass someone on the golf course. □ *Do you mind if we play through? We have to get back to the courtroom by two o'clock.*

plod along to move along slowly but deliberately. □ *I'm just plodding along, but I am getting the job done.* □ *The old man plodded along, hardly able to stand.*

plonk something **down**† to slap something down; to plop something down. □ *He plonked a dollar down and demanded a newspaper.*

plot something **out**† to map something out; to outline a plan for something. □ *I have an idea about how to remodel this room. Let me plot it out for you.*

plow something **up**† to uncover something by plowing. □ *The farmer plowed some old coins up and took them to the museum to find out what they were.*

plug something **up**† to stop or fill up a hole, crack, or gap. □ *Take out the nail and plug the hole up with something.*

plump something **up**† to pat or shake something like a pillow into a fuller shape. □ *He plumped up his pillow.*

plunk (oneself) **down** to sit or fall down hard. □ *Nancy pulled up a chair and plunked herself down.* □ *She plunked herself down in the middle of the kids and began to sing.*

point something **up**† **1.** *Fig.* to emphasize something; to emphasize one aspect of something. □ *This is a very important thing to learn. Let me point it up one more time by drawing this diagram on the board.* **2.** *Fig.* to tuck-point something; to repair the joints in masonry. □ *I hired someone to point the chimney up.*

polish something **off**† to eat, consume, exhaust, or complete all of something. □ *Who polished the cake off?*

polish something **up**† to rub something until it shines. □ *Polish the silver up and make it look nice and shiny.*

poop out *Inf.* to quit; to wear out and stop. □ *He pooped out after about an hour of hard work.*

pop off 1. *Sl.* to make an unnecessary remark; to interrupt with a remark; to sound off. □ *Bob keeps popping off when he should be listening.* **2.** *Sl.* to lose one's temper. □ *Now, don't pop off. Keep your cool.* □ *I don't know why she popped off at me. All I did was say hello.* **3.** *Sl.* to die. □ *My uncle popped off last week.* □ *I hope I'm asleep when I pop off.* **4.** *Sl.* to leave; to depart in haste. □ *Got to pop off. I'm late.*

pop something up† to remove something by making it jump or burst upwards. □ *Henry popped the lid up and helped himself to the strawberry preserves.*

portion something out† to give out shares of something. □ *Who will portion the cake out?* □ *She portioned out the chocolate carefully, making sure everyone got an equal share.*

post something up† to record a transaction in an account. □ *I'll post this charge up right away, and then you can check out.*

pot something up† to put plants into pots. □ *If you would like one of these tomato plants, I'll pot one up for you.*

pound something out† **1.** *Lit.* to flatten something by pounding. □ *He pounded the gold leaf out very thin.* □ *He pounded out the gold leaf.* **2.** *Fig.* to play something loudly on the piano, perhaps with difficulty or clumsily. □ *Here, pound this one out. A little softer, please.* **3.** *Fig.* to type something on a keyboard. □ *I have finished writing it. Can I borrow your laptop so I can pound it out?*

pound something **up**† to break something up by pounding. □ *Pound the crackers up into crumbs and use them to coat the chicken before you fry it.*

power something **up**† to start something, such as an engine. □ *You should power the engine up and let it run awhile before you drive away.*

power up to start an engine. □ *Well, let's power up so we will be ready to leave with the others.*

prance around to dance, jump, or strut around. □ *Stop prancing around and get to work.*

press forward to move forward; to struggle forward; to continue. □ *Do not be discouraged. Let us press forward.*

press something **together** to use pressure to close or unite things. □ *He pressed his lips together and would say no more.*

pretty oneself or something **up**† *Rur.* to make oneself or something more attractive; to tidy oneself or something up. □ *I tried to pretty myself up for him, but he didn't notice.*

price something **down**† to lower the price of something. □ *When they start pricing this stuff down at the end of the season, I'll come in and buy something.*

price something **out** to list and total all the component prices of goods and services for a complex project. □ *I have finished listing all the materials required for the project, and now I have to price it out so that we can decide if we can afford it.*

primp (oneself**) up** to get dressed up; to fix oneself up by combing, brushing, adjusting, etc. □ *Let me stop in the powder room and primp myself up a bit.*

print something **up**† to set something in type and print it; to print something by any process. □ *This looks OK to me. Let's print it up now.*

prune something **away**† to cut away something unwanted or unneeded. □ *Please prune the lower branches of the trees away. They are starting to annoy pedestrians.*

pry something **up**† to raise something with or as with a lever. □ *See if you can pry that trapdoor up.*

psych someone **out**† 1. *Inf.* to get someone very excited; to cause someone to lose mental control. □ *Wow! What you just said really psyched me out!* 2. *Inf.* to figure someone out; to know how someone thinks. □ *It took me a while to psych out Fred, but I have him figured out now.*

psych someone **up**† *Inf.* to get someone excited or mentally prepared for something. □ *I psyched myself up to sing in front of all those people.*

psych up *Inf.* to get mentally ready for something. □ *I have to psych up before the big game tonight.* □ *We want to psych up so we can play a good game.*

pucker up 1. *Lit.* to tighten one's lips together into a circle as if to kiss. □ *He puckered up and kissed her once, and then again.* 2. *Fig.* [for something] to shrink up and get wrinkled. □ *The top edge of the drapes puckered up and I don't know how to straighten it out.*

puff out to swell out. □ *The frog's throat puffed out, and we expected to hear a croak.*

puff someone or something **up**† to boost or promote someone or something. □ *Judy puffed Nell up so much that Nell could not begin to live up to her reputation.*

puff something **out**† to cause something to swell out or expand outward. □ *The frog puffed its throat out and croaked.* □ *The frog puffed out its throat and croaked a mighty croak.*

puff up to swell up. □ *Her finger puffed up and she thought she might have an infection.* □ *His eyelids had puffed up during the night.*

pull oneself **together 1.** *Fig.* to compose oneself; to gather one's wits about one. □ *I have to pull myself together and try it again.* □ *Now try to pull yourself together and get through this crisis.* **2.** *Fig.* to gather up one's things; to pull one's things together. □ *I'll be ready to leave as soon as I pull myself together.*

pull someone **aside**† to grasp and pull a person to one side. □ *I pulled aside the child to say something to him.*

pull someone **down**† *Fig.* to degrade someone; to humiliate someone. □ *I'm afraid that your so-called friends are pulling you down behind your back.*

pull someone or something **apart**† to separate or dismember someone or something. □ *The murderer pulled his victim apart and sought to dispose of the parts.* □ *He pulled apart his victim.*

pull someone or something **up**† to drag or haul someone or something upward or to an upright position. □ *Bob had slipped down into the creek, so I reached down and pulled him up.* □ *I pulled up Bob and nearly fell in myself.*

pull something **down**† **1.** to demolish something; to raze something. □ *Why do they want to pull the building down? Why not remodel it?* □ *They are going to pull down the old building today.* **2.** to lower or reduce the amount of something. □ *That last test pulled my grade down.*

pull something **off**† 1. *Inf.* to manage to make something happen. □ *Yes, I can pull it off.* □ *Do you think you can pull off this deal?* 2. AND **pull** something **off (of)** someone or something *Lit.* to tug or drag something off someone or something else. (*Of* is usually retained before pronouns.) □ *Sam pulled the covers off the bed and fell into it, dead tired.* □ *He pulled off his clothes and stepped into the shower.*

pull something **on**† to draw on an article of clothing. □ *He pulled on his pants quickly and ran outside while putting on his shirt.*

pull something **to** to close something, usually a door of some type. □ *The door is open a little. Pull it to so no one will hear us.*

pump something **up**† 1. to inflate something. □ *Do you have something with which I can pump my basketball up?* □ *I pumped up the ball just an hour ago.* 2. *Sl.* to exercise to make muscles get bigger and stronger. □ *The bodybuilder pumped her muscles up in preparation for the competition.*

punch in to record one's arrival at one's workplace at a certain time. □ *What time did you punch in?*

punch out to record that one has left one's workplace at a certain time. □ *Why didn't you punch out when you left last night?*

punch someone **out**† *Sl.* to overcome or beat someone by punching. □ *He threatened to punch me out.* □ *The thug punched out the cop and ran down an alley.*

punch something **down**† to press something down. □ *Punch this lever down and then try to place your telephone call.*

punch something **in**† to crush or smash something in. □ *Who punched in the cereal box?*

punch something **up**† to register a figure on a cash register or calculator. □ *Jake punched the total up, and the register drawer opened.*

purse something **up**† to bunch or pucker something up. (Usually the lips.) □ *When he tasted the lemon juice, he pursed his lips up and spat it out.*

push out to spread out; to expand outward. □ *His little tummy pushed out when he was full.*

push someone or something **aside**† to shove someone or something to one side. □ *Martha pushed Bill aside and went in ahead of him.*

push someone or something **down**† to force someone or something downward. □ *Every time he tried to get up, the other boys pushed him down again.*

push someone or something **forward** to shove or move someone or something to the front. □ *Mary's mother pushed her forward where she would be seen.*

push someone or something **over**† to make someone or something fall over or fall down. □ *When you ran into me, you nearly pushed me over.*

push someone or something **up**† to raise or lift someone or something. □ *Jake is sliding down again. Push him up.* □ *Push up the window, please.*

push something **in**† to crush something in; to make something cave in. □ *He ran at the door and pushed it in.* □ *He pushed in the door.*

push something **to** to close or nearly close something, such as a door. □ *The door is open a little. Please push it to.* □ *Todd came in and pushed the door to.*

put an animal **down**† *Euph.* to take the life of an animal mercifully. □ *We put down our old dog last year.* □ *It's kind to put fatally ill animals down.*

put an animal **out**† to send an animal, such as a pet, outdoors. □ *Did you put the cat out?* □ *Yes, I put out the cat.*

put one's **feet up**† to sit down, lean back, and rest; to lie down. □ *He was really exhausted and had to go put his feet up.*

put one's **hair up**† to arrange one's hair into a ponytail, bun, etc. (with curlers, hairpins, etc.). □ *I can't go out because I just put my hair up.*

put one's **hand up**† to raise one's hand to get attention from whomever is in charge. □ *The student put his hand up to ask a question of the teacher.*

put oneself **out** to inconvenience oneself. □ *I just don't know why I put myself out for you!*

put out to generate [lots of something]. □ *What a great machine. It really puts out!*

put roots down† (some place) to settle down somewhere; to make a place one's permanent home. □ *I'm not ready to put roots down anywhere yet.* □ *I'm ready to put down roots some place.*

put someone **away**† **1.** *Sl.* to kill someone. (Underworld.) □ *The gangster threatened to put me away if I told the police.* **2.** *Euph.* to bury someone. □ *My uncle died last week. They put him away on Saturday.* **3.** AND **send** someone **away** *Euph.* to have someone put into a mental institution. □ *My uncle became irrational, and they put him away.* **4.** AND **send** someone **away** *Euph.* to sentence someone to prison for a length of time. (Underworld.) □ *They put Richard away for fifteen years.* □ *The judge put away the whole gang.*

put someone **off**† **1.** to delay dealing with someone until a later time. □ *I hate to keep putting you off, but we are not ready to deal with you yet.* **2.** to repel someone; to distress someone. □ *You really put people off with your scowling face.* □ *You put off people with your arrogance.* **3.** to avoid or evade someone. □ *I don't wish to see Mr. Brown now. Please put him off.* □ *I won't talk to reporters. Tell them something that will put them off.*

put someone or something **down**† *Fig.* to belittle or degrade someone or something. □ *It's an old car, but that's no reason to put it down.*

put someone or something **over** to succeed in making someone or something be accepted. □ *Do you think we can put this new product over?*

put someone **out**† to distress or inconvenience someone. □ *I'd like to have a ride home, but not if it puts you out.*

put someone's **eye out**† to puncture or harm someone's eye and destroy its ability to see. □ *Careful with that stick or you'll put your eye out.*

put someone **under** *Fig.* to anesthetize someone. □ *They put him under with ether.*

put someone **up**† to provide lodging for someone. □ *I hope I can find someone to put me up.*

put someone **up**† **(for** something**)** to nominate or offer someone for some office or task. □ *I put Henry up for club president.*

put something **aside**† to set or place something to the side. □ *I put the magazine aside and began reading a book.*

put something **away**† **1.** *Lit.* to return something to its proper storage place. □ *When you are finished with the hammer, please put it away. Don't leave it out.* **2.** *Fig.* to eat something. □ *Are you going to put this last piece of cake away?* □ *Did you put away that whole pizza?*

put something **back**† to return something to where it was before. □ *Please put the book back when you finish it.* □ *Put back the book when you finish.*

put something **down**† *Fig.* to repress or put a stop to something such as a riot or rebellion. □ *The army was called to put down the rebellion.* □ *The police used tear gas to put the riot down.*

put (something) **forth** to exert effort. □ *You are going to have to put more effort forth if you want to succeed.*

put something **forward**† to state an idea; to advance an idea. □ *Toward the end of the meeting, Sally put an idea forward.*

put something **in**† to submit something, such as an order, request, or demand. □ *I put in a request for a new monitor.*

put something **off**† to postpone something; to schedule something for a later time. □ *I put off a visit to the dentist as long as I could.*

put something **on**† to place clothing onto one's body; to get into a piece of clothing. □ *I put a heavy coat on to go outside in the cold.*

put something **on** someone or an animal to clothe someone or an animal in something. □ *The mother put a little jacket on her child.*

145

put something **out**† **1.** to emit something. □ *The factory put a lot of fumes out.* **2.** to extinguish something on fire. □ *He used flour to put the grease fire out.* **3.** to manufacture or produce something. □ *That factory puts electrical supplies out.* □ *We put out some very fine products.* **4.** to publish something. □ *When was this book put out?*

put something **over**† to accomplish something; to put something across. (See also put someone or something **over**.) □ *This is a very hard thing to explain to a large audience. I hope I can put over the main points.*

put something **together 1.** *Lit.* to assemble something. □ *How long will it take to put dinner together?* □ *This model was put together incorrectly.* **2.** *Fig.* to consider some facts and arrive at a conclusion. □ *I couldn't put everything together to figure out the answer in time.*

put something **up**† **1.** to build a building, a sign, a fence, a wall, etc. □ *We'll put a garage up next month.* □ *The city put up a fence next to our house.* **2.** to store and preserve food by canning or freezing. □ *This year we'll put some strawberries up.*

put the heat on† to turn on central heating; to increase the amount of heat in a room or house. □ *It's going to get cold tonight. I'd better put the heat on.* □ *Let's put on the heat to take off the chill.*

put weight on† *Fig.* to gain weight; to grow fat. □ *The doctor says I need to put some weight on.*

puzzle something **out**† to figure something out. □ *I can't puzzle out the meaning of this argument.*

queue up (for something**)** to line up for something. (Typically British.) □ *We had to queue up for tickets to the play.*

quiet down to become quiet; to become less noisy. □ *Please quiet down.*

quiet someone or an animal **down**† to make someone or an animal more quiet. □ *Please go and quiet the children down.* □ *Try to quiet down the children.*

quiz out (of something**)** to earn permission to waive a college course by successful completion of a quiz or exam. □ *Andrew was able to quiz out of calculus.*

R

race around to run or move around in a great hurry. □ *Stop racing around and calm down!*

rack out *Sl.* to go to bed and to sleep. □ *I'm really tired. I've got to go rack out for a while.*

rack something **up**† **1.** *Lit.* to place something onto or into its rack. □ *You had better rack the billiard balls up when you finish this game.* **2.** *Fig.* to accumulate something; to collect or acquire something. □ *They all racked a lot of profits up.* □ *We racked up twenty points in the game last Saturday.* **3.** *Sl.* to wreck or damage something. □ *Fred racked his new car up.*

raffle something **off**† to give something away by a drawing or raffle. □ *They are going to raffle off a television set this weekend at the school.*

rain something **down**† **(on** someone or something**)** to pour something, such as criticism or praise, onto someone or something. (Based on **rain down on** someone or something.) □ *The employees rained criticism down on the personnel manager for the new policy on sick leave.*

rain something **out**† [for the weather] to spoil something by raining. □ *It's starting to sprinkle now. Do you think it will rain out the ball game?*

rake something in (sense 2)

raise someone or something **up**† to lift someone or something up. □ *The aides raised the patient up while the nurse spread clean linen beneath him.*

raise up to lift oneself up; to get up or begin to get up. □ *She raised up and then fell back onto her bed. She was too weak to get up.*

rake something **around**† to spread something around with a rake. □ *She raked the leaves around, spreading them over the flower beds as natural fertilizer.*

rake something **in**† **1.** *Lit.* to draw or pull something inward with a rake. □ *Jane is raking in the leaves into a big pile.* **2.** *Fig.* to take in a lot of something, usually money. □ *Our candidate will rake votes in by the thousand.*

rake something **off**† to steal or embezzle a portion of a payment or an account. □ *They claimed that no one was raking anything off and that the money was only mislaid.*

149

rake something **up**† **1.** *Lit.* to gather and clean up something with a rake. □ *Would you please rake these leaves up before it rains?* □ *Please rake up the leaves.* **2.** to clean something up by raking. □ *Would you rake the yard up?* **3.** *Fig.* to find some unpleasant information. □ *His opposition raked an old scandal up and made it public.*

ram something **down**† to pack something down by pounding, as with a ram. □ *The worker used a pole to ram the earth down and pack it tight.*

rank someone **(out**†**) 1.** *Sl.* to annoy someone. □ *He really ranks me out. What a pest!* **2.** *Sl.* to chastise someone. □ *She ranked him out for being a coward.*

rap something **out**† **(on** something**)** to tap out the rhythm of something on something. □ *Try to rap the rhythm out on the table.*

rasp something **out**† to carve or smooth something out with a rasp. □ *Rasp out the inside carefully.*

ration something **out**† **(among** someone**)** to give people limited shares of something, attempting to make it last as long as possible. □ *The captain rationed the water out among all the crew, trying to make it last as long as possible.*

reach down to extend downward. □ *The stems of the plant reached down almost to the floor.*

reach out 1. *Lit.* to extend one's grasp outward. □ *He reached out, but there was no one to take hold of.* **2.** *Fig.* to enlarge one's circle of friends and experiences. □ *If you are that lonely, you ought to reach out. Get to know some new friends.*

reach something **down**† *Inf.* to hand something down. □ *Please reach the hammer down to me.*

read someone **out**† **(for** something) to chastise someone verbally for doing something wrong. □ *The coach read the player out for making a silly error.*

read something **off**† to read aloud from a list. □ *Nick read the list of the names off, and I wasn't on the list.*

read something **out**† to read something aloud. □ *Please read it out so everyone can hear you.*

read something **over**† to read something. □ *When you have a chance, read this over.*

read something **through**† to read all of something. □ *Take this home and read it through.*

ream someone **out**† *Sl.* to scold someone severely. □ *The teacher really reamed him out.*

ream something **out**† to widen or clean an interior cavity or channel by scraping, grinding, or drilling. □ *Ream the opening out so the flow will be faster.*

rear back 1. *Lit.* [for a horse] to pull back and up onto its hind legs in an effort to move backward rapidly or throw a rider. □ *The animal reared back in terror.* **2.** *Fig.* [for a person] to pull back and stand up or sit up straighter. □ *He reared back in his chair and looked perturbed.*

rear up 1. *Lit.* [for a horse] to lean back on its hind legs and raise its front legs, assuming a threatening posture or avoiding something on the ground such as a snake. □ *When the horse reared up, I almost fell off.* **2.** *Fig.* [for something, especially a problem] to raise up suddenly. □ *A new problem reared up and cost us a lot of time.*

reason something **out**† to figure something out; to plan a reasonable course of action. □ *Now let's be calm and try to reason this out.*

reef a sail **in**† to reduce the area of a ship's sail, by folding the sail. □ *The first mate ordered the sailors to reef the sails in.*

reel something **in**† to bring in something, such as a fish, by winding up the line on a reel. □ *With great effort, she reeled the huge fish in.*

rein someone or something **in**† to bring someone or something under control; to slow down or hold back someone or something. □ *Fred is getting out of hand. The boss undertook to rein him in a bit.* □ *The boss is trying to rein in Jane's enthusiasm.*

rein something **up**† to bring something, usually a horse, to a stop. □ *She reined her horse up and stopped for a chat.* □ *Rein up your horse and stop for a while.*

rein up [for a horse rider] to stop. □ *The equestrian reined up and dismounted.* □ *We all reined up and waited for the cars to pass by.*

remain behind to stay at a place even when others have left. □ *Can't I go too? Do I have to remain behind?*

remain together to stay close together; to stay in association. □ *We will have to remain together while we are on this tour. It is very easy to get lost in this town.*

remain up to stay awake and out of bed. □ *I remained up throughout most of the night.*

render something **down**† **1.** *Lit.* to cook the fat out of something. □ *Polly rendered the chicken fat down to a bit of golden grease that she would use in cooking a special dish.* □ *Jane rendered down the fat for use later.* **2.** *Fig.* to reduce or simplify something to its essentials. □ *Let's render this problem down to the considerations that are important to us.* □ *Can't we render down this matter into its essentials?*

rent something **(out†) (to** someone) to sell temporary rights for the use of something to someone. □ *I like to rent the back room out to a nice young student.* □ *We rented the back room to someone.*

report in to present oneself; to make one's presence known. □ *He reported in and his name was taken off the absentee list.*

rev something **up†** to make an idling engine run very fast, in short bursts of power. □ *I wish that Tom wouldn't sit out in front of our house in his car and rev up his engine.*

rev up to increase in amount or activity. □ *We're hoping business will rev up soon.*

ride away to depart, riding a bike or a horse or similar animal. □ *They rode away without saying good-bye.*

ride off to depart, riding something such as a horse or a bicycle. □ *Betty said good-bye and rode off.*

ride on to continue to ride, traveling onward. □ *We rode on for at least an hour before finding a rest stop.*

ride someone or an animal **down†** to chase down someone or an animal while riding horseback. □ *The mounted policeman rode the mugger down and captured him.* □ *The rider rode down the thief.*

ride something **down** to ride on something that is going down, such as an elevator. □ *I don't want to ride the cable car down. I will walk.*

ride something **out†** to endure something unpleasant. (Originally referred to ships lasting out a storm.) □ *It was a nasty situation, but the mayor tried to ride it out.*

rig something **up†** to prepare something, perhaps on short notice or without the proper materials. □ *We don't have *what's needed to make the kind of circuit you have described, but I think we can rig something up anyway.*

rile someone **up**[†] to get someone excited and angry. □ *He riles up everyone he talks to.*

ring back to call back on the telephone. □ *She's not here now. I suggest you ring back after dinner.*

ring out [for a loud sound] to go out. □ *The bells rang out at the end of the wedding ceremony.* □ *Loud cheers rang out at the end of the game.*

ring someone **back**[†] to call someone back on the telephone. □ *I will have to ring back the store at a later time.*

ring someone **up**[†] to call someone on the telephone. □ *I have to ring up a whole list of people.*

ring something **up**[†] to record the cost of an item on a cash register. □ *Please ring this chewing gum up first, and I'll put it in my purse.*

ring the curtain up[†] **1.** *Fig.* to raise the curtain in a theater. (Alludes to sending the signal to raise the curtain.) □ *The stagehand rang the curtain up precisely on time.* **2.** *Fig.* to start a series of activities or events. □ *I am set to ring up the curtain on a new lifestyle.*

rinse someone or something **down**[†] to wash or clean someone or something with water or other fluid. □ *I rinsed him down for an hour and still didn't get the smell of skunk off him.*

rinse someone or something **off**[†] to wash or clean someone or something by flushing with water or other fluid. □ *Mother rinsed the baby off and dried him with a soft towel.*

rinse someone's **mouth out**[†] **(with soap)** AND **wash** someone's **mouth out**[†] **(with soap)** *Fig.* to punish one by washing one's mouth out with soap, especially for using foul language. (Usually a jocular threat.) □ *If you say that again, I'll rinse your mouth out with soap.*

rinse something **down**† **(with** something**)** to wash something down one's throat with a liquid; to follow something that one has eaten with a drink to aid its going down. □ *Alice rinsed the cheeseburger down with a milk-shake.*

rinse something **out**† **1.** to clean cloth or clothing partially by immersing it in water and squeezing it out. □ *Can you please rinse this rag out? It's all dirty.* **2.** to launder something delicate, such as feminine underwear, using a mild soap. □ *After I rinse out some things, I will be right with you.* **3.** to clean the inside of a container partially by flushing it out with water. □ *Rinse the bottle out and throw it away.*

rip off [for something] to tear or peel off. □ *My pocket ripped off, and my money is gone now!*

rip someone **off**† *Inf.* to steal [something] from someone; to cheat someone. □ *That merchant ripped me off!*

rip someone or something **apart**† to tear someone or something apart into pieces. □ *The automobile accident ripped the car apart.*

rip someone or something **up**† to tear someone or something into bits; to mutilate someone or something. □ *Careful! That machine will rip you up if you fall in.*

rip something **down**† to tear something down. (Alludes to something that has been posted or mounted.) □ *The custodian ripped all the posters down at the end of the day.*

rip something **off**† *Inf.* to steal something [from someone]. □ *The mugger ripped my purse off of me.* □ *Jane ripped off a lot of money.*

rip something **up**† to take something up by force and remove it. (Usually refers to something on the floor or ground, such as carpeting or pavement.) □ *They are going to rip all the broken sidewalk up.*

rise up 1. to come up; to ascend. □ *The water is rising up fast. You had better get to higher ground.* **2.** to get up from lying down. □ *The deer rose up and darted off into the woods.*

roar away to speed away, making a loud clamor. □ *The car roared away into the night with tires screeching.*

roll about to move about, turning or rotating, as a wheel or a ball. □ *The ball rolled about a while and then came to rest.*

roll along 1. *Lit.* [for wheels or something on wheels] to move along, smoothly and rapidly. □ *The wheels of the cart rolled along, making a grinding noise as they went.* **2.** *Fig.* [for something] to progress smoothly. □ *The project is rolling along nicely.*

roll around to move about, rotating, turning over, turning, or moving on wheels. □ *The baby rolled around on the floor, giggling and cooing.*

roll away to move away, rotating, turning over, turning, or moving on wheels. □ *The cart rolled away, and we had to chase it down the hill.*

roll back [for something] to return, rotating or turning or moving on wheels. □ *I rolled the ball away, thinking it would roll back. It didn't.*

roll by 1. *Lit.* to pass by, rotating, as a wheel or a ball; to move past, rolling on wheels. □ *The wheel of a car rolled by, all by itself. It must have come off a car somewhere down the road.* □ *The traffic rolled by relentlessly.* **2.** *Fig.* to move (past), as if rolling. □ *The years rolled by, and soon the two people were old and gray.*

roll down to move downward, rotating, as a wheel or a ball, or to move downward on wheels. □ *I pushed the wagon up the driveway, and it rolled down again.*

roll in *Fig.* to come in large numbers or amounts, easily, as if rolling. (Alludes to the arrival of many wheeled conveyances.) □ *We didn't expect many people at the party, but they just kept rolling in.*

roll on 1. *Lit.* [for something] to continue rolling. □ *The cart came rolling down the hill and rolled on for a few yards at the bottom.* **2.** *Lit.* [for something] to be applied by rolling. □ *This kind of deodorant just rolls on.* □ *She rolled on too much paint and it dripped from the ceiling.* **3.** *Fig.* [for something, such as time] to move on slowly and evenly, as if rolling. □ *The years rolled on, one by one.*

roll one's **sleeves up**† **1.** *Lit.* to turn one's sleeves upward, exposing the arms. □ *He rolled his sleeves up and began to wash the dishes.* **2.** *Fig.* to prepare to get to work. □ *Let's roll our sleeves up and get this job done!*

roll over to turn over; to rotate one half turn. □ *The old man rolled over and started snoring again.*

roll something **away**† to cause something to move away, rotating, turning over, turning, or moving on wheels. □ *Jane rolled the ball away and it was lost.*

roll something **back**† to return something to someone by rotating it, as with a wheel or a ball, or moving it back on wheels. □ *I intercepted the ball and rolled it back.*

roll something **down**† **1.** to move something down, making it rotate like a wheel or a ball, or moving it on wheels. □ *Don't carry the ball down; roll it down!* **2.** to crank down something, such as a car window. □ *Please roll the window down and get some air in this car.*

roll something **in**† to bring something in by rotating it like a wheel or a ball or by moving it on wheels. □ *She put the round table on its edge and rolled it in. Then she went out and got the chairs before the rain started.*

roll something **out**† **1.** to bring or take something out by rolling it; to push something out on wheels. □ *Jane rolled her bike out to show it off.* **2.** to flatten something by rolling it. □ *You should roll the pastry out first.* □ *They rolled out the steel in a huge mill.*

roll something **over**† *Fig.* to renew a financial instrument as it expires. □ *Are you going to roll over your certificates of deposit?*

roll something **up**† to coil or rotate something into a coil or roll of something. □ *I rolled the poster up and put it back in its mailing tube.*

roll something **up**† **(into** something**) 1.** to include something into something that is being rotated into a coil. □ *I guess I accidentally rolled the letter up into the poster that was lying on my desk.* **2.** to make something into a round shape by rolling it. □ *He rolled the gum up into a ball and tossed it away.*

romp around to run and bounce around playfully. □ *The horses were in the meadow, romping around in the crisp autumn air.*

roof something **over**† to build a roof over something; to provide something with a roof. □ *After the destructive storm they had to roof the shed over so that the cow would have some shelter.*

room together [for two or more people] to share a room, as in a college dormitory. □ *Sarah and I roomed together in college.*

root something **out**† to get rid of something completely; to destroy something to its roots or core. □ *No government will ever root out crime completely.*

root something **up**† [for a pig] to find something in the ground by digging with its nose. □ *The pigs will root your plants up if they get out of their pen.*

rope someone or an animal **up**† to tie someone or an animal up with a rope. □ *Rope this guy up tight so he won't get away.*

rope something **off**† to isolate something with a rope barrier. □ *The police roped the scene of the accident off.*

rot away to decompose; to decompose and fall away. □ *The fallen trees rotted away and surrendered their nutrients to the soil.*

rot off to decompose. □ *If you don't clean and repaint that old windowsill, it will rot off.*

rot out to decompose and fall out. □ *If you don't clean your teeth regularly, they'll rot out!*

rough someone **up**† to beat someone up; to maltreat someone. □ *Am I going to have to rough you up, or will you cooperate?*

rough something **in**† to construct or draw something initially, temporarily, or crudely. □ *The carpenter roughed the doorways in without consulting the plans.*

rough something **out**† to make a rough sketch of something. □ *I will rough it out and have one of the staff artists attend to the details.*

rough something **up**† to scrape or rub something in a way that makes it rough. □ *All you have to do is rough the ground up, sow the seeds, and then water them.*

round someone or something **up**† to locate and gather someone or something. □ *The police rounded up the two possible suspects.*

round something **down**† to reduce a fractional part of a number to the next lowest whole number. □ *Please round down all figures having fractions less than one-half.*

round something **off**† to change a number to the next higher or lower whole number. □ *I rounded off 8.789 to 9.*

round something **off**† **(with** something**)** to finish something with something; to complement something with something. □ *We rounded off the meal with a sinful dessert.*

round something **out**† to complete or enhance something. □ *We will round the evening out with dessert at a nice restaurant.*

round something **up**† **1.** to collect a group of people or things; to organize people or things into a group. □ *See if you can round some helpers up.* **2.** to change a number to the next higher whole number. □ *You should round $65.99 up to $66.*

rub someone **out**† *Sl.* to kill someone. (Underworld.) □ *The gunman was eager to rub somebody out.*

rub something **away**† to remove something by chafing or rubbing. □ *See if you can rub some of the dirt away.*

rub something **in**† *Fig.* to keep reminding one of one's failures; to nag someone about something. □ *I like to rub it in. You deserve it!*

rub something **out**† to obliterate something by rubbing. □ *See if you can rub those stains out.* □ *Rub out the graffiti on the side of the car if you can.*

rub something **up**† to raise something, such as the nap of a rug, by rubbing. □ *When you run the vacuum cleaner across the floor, you rub the nap of the rug up and get the dirt out.*

ruffle something **up**† to raise something, such as feathers, up or outward. □ *The bird ruffled its feathers up and started to preen.*

rule someone or something **out**† to prevent, disqualify, overrule, or cancel someone or something. □ *John's bad temper rules him out for the job.*

rumple someone or something **up**† to bring disorder to someone['s clothing] or something; to wrinkle someone or something. □ *One of the little boys knocked another boy down and rumpled him up.*

run along to leave. □ *I have to run along now. Good-bye.*

run around 1. to run here and there. □ *Why are you running around? Sit down and be quiet.* **2.** to go here and there having meetings or doing errands. □ *I've been running around all day, shopping for the party tonight.*

run away (from someone or something**)** to flee someone or something. □ *Please don't run away from me. I mean you no harm.*

run back to come back, running. □ *She ran to the barn and then ran back.*

run down 1. to come down, running or very quickly; to go down, running or very quickly. □ *I need to talk to you down here. Can you run down?* **2.** [for something] to lose power and stop working. □ *The clock ran down because no one was there to wind it.* □ *The toy ran down and wouldn't go again until it had been wound.* **3.** to become worn or dilapidated. □ *The property was allowed to run down, and it took a lot of money to fix it up.*

run off 1. to flee. □ *The children rang our doorbell and then ran off.* □ *They ran off as fast as they could.* **2.** to have diarrhea. □ *He said he was running off all night.* □ *One of the children was running off and had to stay home from school.* **3.** [for a fluid] to drain away from a flat area. □ *By noon, all the rainwater had run off the playground.*

run on 1. to continue running. □ *I wanted to stop her and ask her something, but she just ran on.* □ *The joggers had a chance to stop and rest, but they just ran on.* **2.** to continue on for a long time. □ *The lecture ran on and bored everyone to tears.*

run over 1. to come by for a quick visit. □ *Can you run over for a minute after work?* □ *I will run over for a minute as soon as I can.* **2.** to overflow. □ *The bathtub ran over and there was water all over the floor.*

run someone in† to arrest one and take one to the police station. □ *The cop ran George in so they could question him extensively.*

run something back† to wind something back to the beginning. □ *Run the tape back and listen to it again.*

run something down† to use something having batteries, a motor, or an engine until it has no more power and it stops. □ *Who ran my electric toothbrush down?*

run something **off**† **1.** to get rid of something, such as fat or energy, by running. □ *The little boys are very excited. Send them outside to run it off.* **2.** to duplicate something, using a mechanical duplicating machine. □ *If the master copy is ready, I will run some other copies off.*

run something **up**† **1.** *Lit.* to raise or hoist something, such as a flag. □ *Harry ran the flag up the flagpole each morning.* **2.** *Fig.* to cause something to go higher, such as the price of stocks or commodities. □ *A rumor about higher earnings ran the price of the computer stocks up early in the afternoon.* **3.** *Fig.* to accumulate indebtedness. □ *I ran up a huge phone bill last month.* □ *Walter ran up a bar bill at the hotel that made his boss angry.* **4.** to stitch something together quickly. □ *She's very clever. I'm sure she can run up a costume for you.*

rush something **off**† **(to someone or something)** to send something quickly to someone or something. □ *I will rush your order off to you immediately.*

rust away to dissolve away into rust. □ *In a few years, this car will rust away if you don't take care of it.*

rust out to develop holes or weak places owing to rust. □ *Our hot water heater rusted out and flooded the basement.*

rustle something **up**† *Rur.* to manage to prepare a meal, perhaps on short notice. □ *I think I can rustle something up for dinner.*

S

sack something **up**† to put something into bags or sacks. □ *Please sack the groceries up and put them in the cart.*

saddle an animal **up**† to put a saddle on a horse or some other beast of burden. □ *Please saddle my horse up. I have to leave.*

saddle up 1. *Lit.* to prepare one's horse for riding by putting a saddle on it. □ *Let's saddle up and go for a ride.* **2.** *Fig.* to mount one's horse and sit in the saddle. □ *The cowboys saddled up and took off after the rustlers.*

sail around to travel by water in a boat or ship. □ *We sailed around for about an hour and then went back to the shore.*

sally forth to go forth; to leave and go out. □ *The soldiers sallied forth from behind the stone wall.*

salt something **away**† **1.** *Lit.* to store and preserve a foodstuff by salting it. □ *The farmer's wife salted a lot of fish and hams away for the winter.* **2.** *Fig.* to store something; to place something in reserve. □ *I need to salt some money away for my retirement.*

salt something **down**† to place salt on something, such as icy roads. □ *I won't go out until midmorning, after they have salted the roads down.*

sand something **down**† **1.** to make something smooth by rubbing it with sandpaper. (To act on the main body of the object, not the imperfections.) □ *You should sand the board down before you paint it.* **2.** to remove bumps or imperfections on the surface of something by rubbing them with sandpaper. (To act on the imperfections, not the main body of the object.) □ *Sand these bumps down, will you?*

save money up† **(for** something) to accumulate or amass an amount of money for the purchase of something. □ *I'm saving my money up for a car.*

save something **up**† to save something; to accumulate something. □ *If you'd only save your money up, you could buy anything you want.*

saw something **down**† to cut something down with a saw. □ *We are going to have to saw that dead tree down before it falls on the house.*

scab over [for a wound] to form a scab. □ *The wound soon scabbed over and the injury was well on its way to healing.*

scale something **down**† to reduce the size or cost of something. □ *The bad economy forced us to scale the project down.*

scamper along [for a child or small animal] to run along nimbly. □ *The rabbit scampered along, unaware that a fox was following it.*

scamper away [for a child or small animal] to run away nimbly. □ *The rabbit scampered away across the lawn.* □ *The children scampered away when they heard the teacher coming.*

scare someone or an animal **off**† to frighten someone or an animal away. □ *The dog's barking scared the burglar off.*

scare someone or something **up**† *Rur.* to search for and find someone or something. □ *Go out in the kitchen and scare some food up.*

scoop something **up**† to gather and remove something by scooping, dipping, or bailing. □ *Karen scooped the nuts up and put them in a bag.*

scour something **out**† to clean something out by scouring. □ *Please scour out the pans—don't just wash them.*

scout someone or something **out**† to search for and discover someone or something. □ *I will scout a new salesclerk out for you if you want.*

scout someone or something **up**† to search for and find someone or something. □ *I'll scout up a costume for the Halloween party.*

scrape something **out**† to empty something by scraping. □ *Scrape the pan out. Don't leave any of that good sauce inside.*

scrape something **together**† to gather things together by scraping. □ *The waiter scraped all the crumbs together and removed them from the table with a little gadget.*

scratch someone or something **out**† to mark out the name of someone or something. □ *I scratched John out and wrote in George instead.*

scratch someone or something **up**† to damage or mar someone or something by scratching. □ *Being thrown clear of the car in the accident didn't break any bones, but it scratched her up a lot.*

scream someone **down**† to scream loudly at someone; to outscream someone. □ *They screamed her down and drove her from the platform.*

screw someone or something **up**[†] *Inf.* to interfere with someone or something; to mess up someone or something. □ *Try again and don't screw it up this time.*

screw someone **up**[†] *Inf.* to confuse someone mentally. □ *Please don't screw me up again!*

screw something **down**[†] to secure something to the floor or a base by the use of screws. □ *You had better screw these seats down or someone will knock them over.*

screw something **up**[†] to attach something to a higher place by the use of screws. □ *The bracket holding the shelf up has come loose. Will you please screw it up again?*

screw up 1. *Inf.* to mess up. □ *I hope I don't screw up this time.* □ *The waiter screwed up again.* **2.** *Inf.* a mess; a blunder; utter confusion. (Usually **screw-up**.) □ *This is the chef's screw-up, not mine.*

scribble something **down**[†] to write something down fast and not too neatly. □ *He scribbled the figure down and raced for the telephone.*

scrounge someone or something **up**[†] *Fig.* to find someone or something somewhere; to dig someone or something up. □ *I can't think of anyone just now, but I will scrounge someone up.*

scrub someone or something **down**[†] to clean someone or something thoroughly by rubbing. □ *The mother scrubbed the baby down gently and put lotion on her.*

scrub someone or something **off**[†] to clean someone or something by rubbing. □ *Mother scrubbed Timmy off.*

scrub something **away**[†] to clean something away by rubbing. □ *See if you can scrub that rust away.*

scrub something **out**† to clean out the inside of something by rubbing or brushing. □ *Please scrub these pots out and put them away.*

scrub up 1. *Lit.* to clean oneself up. □ *You have to scrub up before dinner.* □ *Please go scrub up before you come to the table.* **2.** *Fig.* to clean oneself, especially one's hands and arms, as a preparation for performing a surgical procedure. □ *The surgeon scrubbed up thoroughly before the operation.*

scrunch down to squeeze or huddle down into a smaller shape. □ *Mary scrunched down, trying to hide behind the chair.*

scrunch something **up**† to crush or crunch up. □ *I pounded the biscuits and scrunched them up into crumbs.*

scuff something **up**† to scrape or scratch something. □ *Please don't scuff up my freshly polished floors!*

see someone **off**† to accompany one to the point of departure for a trip and say good-bye upon departure. □ *We went to the train station to see Andy off.*

see something **through** to follow through on something until it is completed. □ *Mary is prepared to see the project through.*

seize something **up**† to grab or take something. □ *The crow seized the freshly hatched chick up and flew away.*

seize up to freeze or halt; to grind suddenly to a stop. □ *The engine seized up, and the car coasted to a stop.*

sell out [for an item] to be sold until there is no more. □ *All the plastic hangers have sold out.*

sell someone **out**† AND **sell** someone **down the river** to betray someone; to reveal damaging information about someone. □ *Bill told everything he knew about Bob, and* *that sold Bob down the river.* □ *You'll be sorry if you sell me out.*

sell something **off**† to sell all of something. □ *We ended up with a large stock of out-of-style coats and we had to sell them all off at a loss.*

sell something **out**† to sell all of something. □ *Have they sold their supply out yet?*

send someone or something **along**† to help someone or something continue along; to send someone. □ *I knew it was time for Johnny to go home, so I sent him along.*

send someone or something **away**† to cause someone, a group, or something to leave. □ *The store sent away all late deliveries.*

send someone or something **back**† to cause someone or something to return. □ *He came to apologize, but I sent him back.*

send someone or something **down**† to dispatch someone or something to some place on a lower level. □ *They wanted someone downstairs to help with the moving, so I sent John down.*

send someone or something **up**† **1.** *Lit.* to order someone to go upward to a higher level; arrange for something to be taken upward to a higher level. □ *They are hungry on the tenth floor. Let's send some sandwiches up.* **2.** *Fig.* to parody or ridicule someone or something. □ *Comedians love to send the president or some other famous person up.*

send someone **up**† *Fig.* to mock or ridicule, particularly by imitation. □ *Last week, he sent the prime minister up.*

serve something **out**† to carry out one's duty or responsibility for the whole time, all the way to the end. □ *She was unable to serve her term out.*

serve something **up**† to distribute or deliver food for people to eat. □ *The cook served the stew up and then passed around the bread.*

set in to begin; to become fixed for a period of time. □ *A severe cold spell set in early in November.*

set someone **off**† **1.** *Fig.* to cause someone to become very angry; to ignite someone's anger. □ *That kind of thing really sets me off!* □ *Your rude behavior set off Mrs. Franklin.* **2.** *Fig.* to cause someone to start talking or lecturing about a particular subject. □ *When I mentioned high taxes it really set Walter off. He talked and talked.*

set someone or something **down**† AND **put** someone or something **down**† to lower or set down someone or something. □ *Put me down!* □ *Please set that vase down. It cost a fortune.*

set someone **up**† to lead—by deception—a person to play a particular role in an event; to arrange an event—usually by deception—so that a specific person suffers the consequences for the event; to frame someone. □ *I had nothing to do with the robbery! I was just standing there. Somebody must have set me up!* □ *John isn't the one who started the fight. Somebody set up the poor guy.*

set something **aside**† to place something in a place that is to one side or out of the way. □ *Betty set the manuscript aside until she had more time to work on it.*

set something **back**† AND **put** something **back**† to set something, like a timepiece, to a lower number. (*Put* is less common.) □ *It's that time of year when you must set* *your clocks and watches back!* □ *Set back your clock tonight.*

set something **down**† AND **put** something **down** **1.** to place something on the surface of something. □ *Andy set the hot skillet down on the dishcloth and burned a hole in it.* **2.** to write something on paper. □ *Let me put this down on paper so we will have a record of what was said.* □ *I will set down this note on paper.* **3.** to land an aircraft. □ *The pilot put the plane down exactly on time.*

set something **forth**† to explain something; to present some information. □ *She set her ideas forth in an organized and interesting manner.*

set something **forward** **1.** to move something to a more forward position. □ *Please set the chair forward a little bit. It is in the walkway.* □ *If you set the vase forward, it will show up better against the dark background.* **2.** to reset a timepiece to a later time. □ *You are supposed to set your clock forward at this time of year.*

set something **off**† **1.** *Lit.* to ignite something, such as fireworks. □ *The boys were setting firecrackers off all afternoon.* □ *They set off rocket after rocket.* **2.** *Fig.* to cause something to begin. □ *The coach set the race off with a shot from the starting pistol.* **3.** *Fig.* to make something distinct or outstanding. □ *The lovely stonework sets the fireplace off quite nicely.*

set something **up** **1.** *Lit.* to put something together; to erect something. □ *My parents bought me a dollhouse, but I had to set it up myself.* **2.** *Fig.* to establish or found something. □ *We set up a fund to buy food for the needy.*

set to to begin to fight; to attack or commence someone or something. □ *The two boys set to almost as soon as they met each other.*

settle down 1. to calm down. □ *Now, children, it's time to settle down and start class.* □ *If you don't settle down, I'll send you all home.* **2.** to settle into a stable way of life; to get married and settle into a stable way of life. □ *Tom, don't you think it's about time you settled down and stopped all of this running around?*

settle in to become accustomed to one's new surroundings; to get used to living in a place or a new dwelling. □ *I need a little time to settle in, then I can think about buying a car.*

sew someone or something **up**† **1.** *Lit.* to stitch together an opening in someone or something. □ *The surgeon sewed the patient up and pronounced the operation a success.* **2.** *Fig.* to complete one's dealings with or discussion of someone or something. □ *It's time to sew this up and go home.* □ *I think we can sew up the shipping contract this afternoon and get on to someone else.*

shake a disease or illness **off**† *Fig.* [for the body] to fight off a disease or illness. □ *I hope I can shake off this flu pretty soon.*

shake someone **down**† **1.** to blackmail someone. (Underworld.) □ *Fred was trying to shake Jane down, but she got the cops in on it.* □ *The police chief was trying to shake down just about everybody in town.* **2.** to put pressure on someone to lend one money. □ *We tried to shake down Max for a few hundred, but no deal.*

shake someone or something **off**† *Fig.* to get rid of someone; to get free of someone who is bothering you. □ *Stop bothering me! What do I have to do to shake you off?*

shake someone or something **up**† to jostle or knock someone or something around; to toss someone or something back and forth. □ *We rode over a rough road, and that shook us up.*

shake someone down (sense 2)

shake someone **up**† to shock or upset someone. □ *The sight of the injured man shook me up.*

shake something **off**† to get rid of something that is on one by shaking. □ *I tried to shake the spider off.* □ *The dog shook off the blanket Billy had put on him.*

shake something **out**† **1.** *Lit.* to clean something of dirt or crumbs by shaking. □ *Can you shake out your coat? It's really dusty.* **2.** AND **shake** something **down**† *Fig.* to test something to find out how it works or what the problems are. □ *I need to spend some time driving my new car to shake it out.* □ *We need to shake down this car before I buy it.*

shake something **up**† **1.** *Lit.* to shake a container to mix its contents together well. □ *Please shake this up before using it.* □ *I shook up the medicine bottle like it says on the label.* **2.** *Fig.* to reorganize a group or organization, not always in a gentle way. □ *The new manager shook the office up and made things run a lot better.*

shape someone **up**† to get someone into good physical shape; to make someone behave or perform better. □ *I've got to shape myself up to improve my health.*

shape up 1. to improve; to reform. □ *I want to get things shaped up around here.* □ *I guess I'd better shape up if I want to stay in school.* **2.** to assume a final form or structure. □ *The game plan for the election was beginning to shape up.*

shook up upset; shocked. □ *Relax, man! Don't get shook up!* □ *I always get shook up when I see a bad accident.*

shoot one's **mouth off**† *Inf.* to boast or talk too much; to tell secrets. □ *Don't pay any attention to Bob. He's always shooting his mouth off.*

shoot something **down**† *Fig.* to foil a plan through criticism; to counter an idea with criticism. □ *He raised a good point, but the others shot him down almost immediately.*

shoot something **out**† **1.** to stick, throw, or thrust something outward. □ *The diamond shot bright shafts of light out when the sun fell on it.* **2.** to settle a matter by the use of guns. □ *Bill and the cowboy—with whom he had been arguing—went out in the street and shot it out.*

shore someone **up**† *Fig.* to prop up or support someone. □ *Mary's solid character and personality helped shore her up during her recent problems with the law.*

shore something **up**† to prop up or support something. □ *The storm weakened the foundation of our house, and we had to have workers shore up the house.*

shout someone or something **down**† to overwhelm someone or something by shouting. □ *Mary was trying to speak, but Sally shouted her down.* □ *Ann brought up a very important suggestion, but Bob shouted it down.*

show off to do things in a way that is meant to attract attention. □ *Please stop showing off! You embarrass me.*

show someone or something **off**† to display someone or something so that the best features are apparent. □ *Bill drove around all afternoon showing his new car off.*

show someone **up**† to make someone's faults or short-comings apparent. □ *John is always trying to show some-one up to make himself look better.*

show up to appear; to arrive. □ *Where is John? I hope he shows up soon.* □ *When will the bus show up?*

shuck something **off**† **1.** to take something off. □ *Tom shucked his jacket off and sat on the arm of the easy chair.* **2.** to get rid of someone or something. □ *She shucked all her bad habits off.*

shut someone **up**† to silence someone. □ *Oh, shut yourself up!* □ *Will you please shut up that crying baby!*

Shut up! *Inf.* Be quiet! (Impolite.) □ *Bob: And another thing. Bill: Oh, shut up, Bob!* □ *Andy: Shut up! I've heard enough! Bob: But I have more to say!*

sign in to indicate that one has arrived somewhere and at what time by signing a piece of paper or a list. □ *Please sign in so we will know you are here.*

sign off 1. *Lit.* [for a broadcaster] to announce the end of programming for the day; [for an amateur radio operator] to announce the end of a transmission. □ *Wally signed off and turned the transmitter off.* **2.** *Fig.* to quit doing what one has been doing and leave, go to bed, quit trying to do something, etc. □ *I have to sign off and get to bed. See you all.*

175

sign on to announce the beginning of a broadcast transmission. □ *The announcer signed on and then played "The Star-Spangled Banner."*

sign out to indicate that one is leaving a place or going out temporarily by signing a piece of paper or a list. □ *I forgot to sign out when I left.*

sign someone **in**† to record that someone has arrived somewhere and at what time by recording the information on a paper or a list. □ *I will sign you in. What is your name?*

sign someone **on**† to employ someone; to recruit someone as an employee. □ *How many workers did the manager sign on?*

sign someone **up**† **(for** something**)** to record the agreement of someone, including oneself, to participate in something. □ *Has anyone signed you up for the office picnic?*

sign someone **up**† **(with** someone or something**)** to record the agreement of someone to join someone, a group of people, or an organization. □ *I want to sign George up with our softball team.*

sign something **away**† to sign a paper in which one gives away one's rights to something. □ *Valerie signed her rights away.*

sign something **in**† to record that something has been received at a particular time by recording the information on a paper or a list. □ *I have to sign this package in, then I will be right with you.*

silt up [for a body of water] to become filled with silt. □ *The river moved too fast to silt up.*

simmer down 1. *Lit.* to decrease in intensity. (As boiling dies down when the heat is lowered or removed.)

□ *When things simmer down in the fall, this is a much nicer place.* **2.** *Fig.* [for someone] to become calm or less agitated. □ *I wish you would simmer down.*

sink down to sink or submerge. □ *The sun sank down and darkness spread across the land.* □ *She sat in the chair and sank down, enjoying her moment of relaxation.*

sink in 1. *Lit.* to sink, submerge, or descend into something. □ *It might take days for the oil to sink in, so you have time to clean it up.* **2.** *Fig.* [for knowledge] to be understood. □ *I pay careful attention to everything I hear in calculus class, but it usually doesn't sink in.*

sit down to be seated; to sit on something, such as a chair. □ *Please sit down and make yourself comfortable.*

sit something **out**† not to participate in something; to wait until something is over before participating. □ *Oh, please play with us. Don't sit it out.*

sit up 1. to rise from a lying to a sitting position. □ *When the alarm went off, he sat up and put his feet on the floor.* □ *She couldn't sleep, so she sat up and read a book.* **2.** to sit more straight in one's seat; to hold one's posture more upright while seated. □ *Please sit up. Don't slouch!*

size someone or something **up**† to observe someone or something to get information. □ *The comedian sized the audience up and decided not to use his new material.* □ *I like to size up a situation before I act.*

skate around to skate here and there in no particular direction. □ *Let's go over to the pond and skate around.*

sketch something **in**† to draw in the image of someone or something. □ *I sketched a figure of a woman in so that she appears to be standing beneath the tree.*

sketch something **out**† to create a rough idea or image of something by sketching or some other means. (Does not necessarily require an actual sketch.) □ *Sally sketched the furniture arrangement out so we could get an idea of what it was to look like.*

slack off 1. to taper off; to reduce gradually. □ *Business tends to slack off during the winter months.* **2.** [for someone] to become lazy or inefficient. □ *Near the end of the school year, Sally began to slack off, and her grades showed it.*

slam someone or something **down**† to drive or strike someone or something downward. □ *The wrestler slammed his opponent down hard.*

slap someone **down**† **1.** *Lit.* to cause someone to fall by striking with the open hand. □ *She became enraged and slapped him down when he approached her again.* **2.** *Fig.* to squelch someone; to rebuke or rebuff someone. □ *I had a great idea, but the boss slapped me down.*

slap something **down**† to strike downward with something flat in one's hand. □ *She slapped the dollar bill down in great anger and took her paper cup full of water away with her.*

slap something **on**† *Inf.* to dress in something hastily. □ *Henry slapped a shirt on and went out to say something to the garbage hauler.*

slash and burn 1. *Lit.* of a farming technique where vegetation is cut down and burned before crops are planted. (Hyphenated before nominals.) □ *The small farmers' slash-and-burn technique destroyed thousands of acres of forest.* **2.** *Fig.* of a crude and brash way of doing something. (Hyphenated before nominals.) □ *The new manager's method was strictly slash and burn.*

He looks decisive to his boss and merciless to the people he fires.

sleep in to oversleep; to sleep late in the morning. □ *If you sleep in again, you'll get fired.*

sleep out to sleep outside or away from one's home. □ *Can I sleep out tonight?*

sleep something **away**[†] to spend or waste a specific period of time sleeping. □ *You can't sleep the whole day away!*

sleep something **off**[†] to sleep while the effects of liquor or drugs pass away. □ *Bill is at home sleeping off the effects of the drug they gave him.*

sleep together 1. [for two or more people] to share a bed. □ *Do you mean that Fred and Dave have to sleep together?* □ *My brother and I used to have to sleep together.* **2.** *Euph.* [for two people] to copulate. □ *Do you think they slept together?*

slice something **off**[†] to cut something off with slicing motions. □ *Sue sliced the dead branches off with a tree saw.*

slick something **down**[†] to brush or comb down hair, usually with some sort of dressing or water. □ *He used something gooey—grease or something—to slick his hair down.*

slick something **up**[†] to tidy up something or some place. □ *I have to slick this house up a little.*

slide along to slip or glide along. □ *The sled slid along at a good clip down the gently sloping hill.*

slide around to slip or skid around. □ *Many cars slide around on the roads when they are icy.*

slide by to get along with a minimum of effort. □ *She didn't do a lot of work—she just slid by.*

slim down to become thinner; to lose weight. □ *You have really slimmed down a lot since I last saw you.* □ *I need to eat less so I can slim down.*

slim someone **down**† to cause someone to lose weight. □ *They started to slim her down in the hospital, but she gained the weight back as soon as she got out.*

sling something **out**† **1.** to toss or heave something outward. □ *The fishermen slung their nets out into the water.* □ *They slung out their nets.* **2.** to throw something away. □ *Just sling all that old junk out, if you will.*

slink around to creep or slither around furtively. □ *Don't slink around like that. Someone is likely to take you for a robber.*

slink away to creep or slither away furtively. □ *The fox slunk away, leaving the henhouse as quietly as such a thing is possible.*

slink off to creep away furtively. □ *Carl was embarrassed and tried to slink off, but the ushers spotted him.*

slip by 1. AND **slip by** someone or something to move by someone or something quickly or unnoticed; to move through a tight area or past someone or something in a tight area. □ *The hall was narrow, and I could hardly have slipped by.* **2.** [for time] to pass quickly or unnoticed. □ *Goodness, almost an hour has slipped by! How time flies.*

slip down to slide or glide downward. □ *His socks kept slipping down.* □ *He lost so much weight that his pants almost slipped down.*

slip out 1. [for someone] to exit quietly without bothering anyone. □ *I slipped out during intermission.* **2.** [for information] to be spoken without realizing that it is secret or privileged. □ *The secret about her divorce slipped out when we were discussing old friends.*

slip something **back**† **1.** to pull or place something back. □ *Alice slipped the gearshift lever back and away they went.* □ *She slipped back the gearshift and sped away.* **2.** to return something secretively. □ *Someone took my wallet away and slipped it back later.*

slip something **down**† to slide something downward. □ *I slipped my pants down a little so the doctor could give me a shot in what they call your "hip."*

slip something **off**† to let an item of clothing slide off one's body; to remove an item of clothing easily or casually. □ *He slipped his coat off and put it on a chair.*

slip up something to climb something, slipping along the way. □ *The hikers slipped up the wet slope.*

slither along to slink or crawl along. □ *The snake slithered along, unmindful of our presence.*

slither away to sneak or crawl away, like a snake. □ *The little lizards slithered away soundlessly.*

slop over [for a liquid] to splash out of or overflow a container. □ *Her cup slopped over and spilled its contents on the kitchen table.*

slosh over [for a liquid] to splash over its container. □ *The water in the wading pool sloshed over and made the grass slippery.*

slosh something **around**† to cause a liquid to rush or splash in a container. □ *The chef sloshed the dressing around a few times and poured it on the salad.*

slouch around to move around with a stooped or bent body. (One may slouch because of age, illness, fatigue, depression, fear, or with the intention of not being observed.) □ *She is slouching around because she is tired.*

slouch down to slump or droop down. □ *Don't always slouch down, Timmy! Stand up straight.*

slouch over to lean or crumple and fall to one side; [for someone] to collapse in a sitting position. □ *He slouched over and went to sleep in his chair.*

slough something **off**† **1.** *Lit.* to brush or rub something off. □ *The snake sloughed its old skin off.* □ *It sloughed off its skin.* **2.** *Fig.* to ignore or disregard a negative remark or incident. □ *I could see that the remark had hurt her feelings, but she just pretended to slough it off.*

slow someone or something **up**† AND **slow** someone or something **down**† to cause someone or something to reduce speed. □ *I'm in a hurry. Don't try to slow me down.* □ *Please slow up the train. There are sheep near the track.*

slow up to go slower; to reduce speed in order for someone or something to catch up. □ *Slow up a little! I can't keep up with you!*

sluice something **down**† to rinse something down; to flood the surface of something with water or other liquid to clean it. □ *John sluiced the driveway down.*

sluice something **out**† to rinse something out; to flood the inside of something to clean it. □ *Sluice the wheelbarrow out, will you?*

slump down [for someone] to collapse and fall down; [for someone] to crumple. □ *The shot hit Max and he slumped down.*

slump over [for someone] to collapse and fall over forward in a sitting position. □ *Just after the gunshot, Bruno slumped over and slid from his chair.*

smack someone **down†** **1.** *Lit.* to knock a person down or cause a person to retreat with a slap or a blow. □ *He tried to touch her again and she smacked him down.* **2.** *Fig.* to rebuke someone. □ *She smacked him down by telling him that he didn't fit in there anymore.* □ *He has a way of smacking down people who ask stupid questions.*

smarten up to get smarter; to become more alert and knowing. □ *You had better smarten up if you want to survive around here.*

smash someone's **face in†** **1.** *Fig.* to crush someone's face. □ *The accident smashed Harry's face in, and he had to have extensive surgery.* **2.** *Inf.* to strike someone in the face. □ *You had better stop that or I will smash your face in.*

smash something **in†** to crush something inward; to make something collapse inward by striking it. □ *Andy gave one good kick and smashed the box in.*

smash something **up†** to break something up; to destroy something. □ *I hope the children don't smash any of the good china up if we use it tonight.*

smell something **up†** to cause a bad or strong odor in a place or on something. □ *Your cooking sure smelled this place up!*

smoke something **up†** to cause something or a place to become smoky. □ *Get out of here with that cigarette! I don't want you smoking my house up!*

smooth something **away†** to remove something, such as wrinkles or other unevenness, by pressing or smooth-

ing. □ *Jeff put the cloth on the table and smoothed the wrinkles away with his hand.*

smooth something **back**† to flatten and position something by pressing or smoothing. □ *He smoothed his hair back out of his eyes.*

smooth something **down**† to make something flat or smooth by pressing. □ *She smoothed her skirt down, fluffed her hair, and went into the boardroom.*

smooth something **out**† **1.** *Lit.* to flatten or even something by smoothing or pressing. □ *Wally smoothed the bedspread out.* □ *Wally finished making the bed by smoothing out the spread.* **2.** *Fig.* to polish and refine something. □ *The editor smoothed John's style out.* **3.** AND **smooth** something **over**† *Fig.* to reduce the intensity of an argument or a misunderstanding; to try to make people feel better about something disagreeable that has happened. (*Fig.* on ①.) □ *Mary and John had a terrible argument, and they are both trying to smooth it over.* □ *Let's get everyone together and try to smooth things out. We can't keep on arguing with one another.*

smuggle someone or something **out of** some place AND **smuggle** someone or something **out**† to move someone or something across a border out of a place illegally and in secret. □ *Judy smuggled her cousin out of the country in a van.*

snake along to move along in a curving line, looking like a snake; to move along in a line, moving as a snake moves. □ *The train snaked along, gaining speed as it went downhill.*

snap someone's **head off** *Fig.* to speak very sharply to someone. □ *How rude! Don't snap my head off!* □ *Mary snapped Ted's head off because he had come in late.*

snap something **back**† to cause something to jerk back. □ *The force of the crash snapped his head back and injured his neck.*

snap something **into** something AND **snap** something **in**† to put or press something into something with an audible snap. □ *Next, you snap this little part into this slot here.*

snap something **off**† to break off something brittle. □ *Liz snapped a bit of the rock off and put it in her bag.*

snap something **on**† to attach something to something else, causing an audible snap. □ *Dawn took two pills from the bottle and snapped the lid on.*

snap something **up**† **1.** *Lit.* to grasp something quickly. □ *Karen snapped her pencil up and strode out of the room.* □ *Harry walked through the kitchen and snapped up two cookies on the way.* **2.** *Fig.* to purchase something quickly, because the price is low or because the item is so hard to find. (Fig. on ①.) □ *We put the cheap shirts out for sale this morning and people snapped them up in only a few minutes.* □ *They snapped up the bargains quickly.* **3.** *Fig.* to believe something eagerly; to believe a lie readily. □ *They are so gullible that you can say anything and they'll snap it up.*

snarl someone or something **up**† to tangle someone or something; to mess something up. □ *The wind snarled my hair up terribly.*

snarl something **out**† to utter something by snarling or growling. □ *Lefty snarled a naughty word out at the police.* □ *Walt the pickpocket snarled out a curse as the cop grabbed his coat collar.*

snatch something **up**† **1.** *Lit.* to grasp something and lift it up. □ *Tom snatched the last cookie up and popped it* *into his mouth.* **2.** *Fig.* to collect or acquire as many of something as possible. □ *The shoppers snatched the sale merchandise up very quickly.*

sniff someone or something **out**† to locate someone or something by sniffing or as if by sniffing. □ *The dog sniffed the intruder out and the police captured him.*

snuff someone **out**† *Sl.* to kill someone. □ *Max really wanted to snuff the eyewiteness out, once and for all.*

snuff something **out**† to extinguish something, such as a flame. □ *She snuffed all the candles out and went to bed.* □ *Karen snuffed out the flames one by one.*

snuggle down (into something) to nestle into something, such as a warm bed. □ *Toby snuggled down into his nice warm bed.*

snuggle down (with someone) to nestle [into something] with someone else. □ *Billy snuggled down with his sister in the big feather bed.*

snuggle down (with something) to nestle [into something] with something, such as a blanket, doll, book, etc. □ *Sally grabbed onto her favorite doll and snuggled down for the night.*

snuggle (up) against someone or something to press or cuddle against someone or something, as if to keep warm. □ *Tiffany snuggled up against Tad and asked him to give her some chewing gum.* □ *He snuggled against the warm wall on the other side of the fireplace.*

snuggle up (to someone or something) to cuddle up close to someone or something. □ *She snuggled up and said she wanted him to go pick up a pizza.*

soak something **up**† **1.** *Lit.* to gather up moisture or a liquid, using an absorbent cloth, paper, etc. □ *Alice soaked* *the spill up with a sponge.* **2.** *Lit.* [for cloth, paper, or other absorbent material] to absorb moisture or a liquid. □ *Please get some paper towels to soak the spill up.* **3.** *Fig.* to learn or absorb some information; to learn much information. □ *I can't soak information up as fast as I used to be able to.* □ *The tourists will soak up anything you tell them.*

soap someone or something **down**† to cover someone or something thoroughly with soap or suds. □ *Mother soaped Timmy down and rinsed him off in warm water.*

sob something **out**† to speak something out while sobbing. □ *Wally sobbed his story out while the police made notes.*

sober someone **up**† **1.** *Lit.* to take actions that will cause a drunken person to become sober. □ *Some coffee ought to sober him up.* □ *He tried to sober himself up because he had to drive home.* **2.** *Fig.* to cause someone to face reality. □ *The harsh reality of what had happened sobered him up immediately.* □ *The arrival of the police sobered up all the revelers.*

sober up to recover from alcohol or drug intoxication. □ *Barlowe had one hour to sober up and get to the station.*

sock someone or something **in**† [for fog] to cause someone or something to remain in place. □ *The heavy fog socked us in for six hours.*

sock something **away**† to place something, such as money, into reserve; to store something in a secure place. □ *I try to sock a little money away each month for my vacation.* □ *I will sock away some money.*

soften someone **up**† *Fig.* to prepare to persuade someone of something. □ *I will talk to Fred and soften him up for your request.*

soften something **up**† to take actions that will make something softer. □ *Soften the butter up before you add it to the batter.*

soften up 1. *Lit.* [for something] to become softer. □ *The candles will probably soften up and bend over in this hot weather.* **2.** *Fig.* [for someone] to adopt a more gentle manner. □ *After a while, she softened up and was more friendly.*

sop something **up**† to mop or soak up a liquid. □ *Use this rag to sop the spilled milk up.*

sort oneself **out** to pull oneself together; to figure out what to do about one's problems. □ *I need a few days to sort myself out.*

sort something **out**† **1.** *Lit.* to sort something; to arrange according to class or category. □ *Let's sort these cards out.* **2.** *Fig.* to study a problem and figure it out. □ *I can't sort this out without some more time.*

sound off to speak something loudly; to call out one's name or one's place in a numerical sequence. □ *All right, sound off, you guys!*

sound someone **out**† to try to find out what someone thinks (about something). □ *I don't know what Jane thinks about your suggestion, but I'll sound her out.*

sound something **out**† to pronounce the letters or syllables of a word as a means of figuring out what the word is. (Usually said to a child.) □ *This word is easy, Bobby. Try to sound it out.*

soup something **up**† to increase the power of something. □ *He souped his car up so it will do nearly 120 miles per hour.* □ *If only I could soup up this computer to run just a little faster.*

space out to become giddy or disoriented. □ *Judy spaced out during the meeting and I didn't understand a word she said.*

space someone **out**† to cause someone to become giddy. □ *The circus clowns just spaced me out.*

spade something **up**† to turn over the soil in a garden plot with a spade. □ *Please go out and spade the garden up so I can plant the potatoes and onions.*

spark something **off**† **1.** *Lit.* to ignite something flammable or explosive. □ *The lightning sparked a fire off.* □ *The match sparked off a raging inferno.* **2.** *Fig.* to cause or start some violent or energetic activity. □ *We were afraid there would be a riot and the speaker nearly sparked it off.*

speak out to speak loudly; to speak to be heard. □ *Please speak out. We need to hear you.*

speak out (on something**)** to say something frankly and directly. □ *This law is wrong, and I intend to speak out on it until it is repealed.* □ *You must speak out. People need to know what you think.*

speak up 1. *Lit.* to speak more loudly. □ *They can't hear you in the back of the room. Please speak up.* □ *What? Speak up, please. I'm hard of hearing.* **2.** *Fig.* to **speak out (on** something**).** □ *If you think that this is wrong, you must speak up and say so.* □ *I'm too shy to speak up.*

speed someone or something **up**† to cause someone or something to move faster. □ *We tried to speed him up, but he is just a very slow person.* □ *We sped up the process, but it still took too long.*

spell someone **down**† to win over someone in a spelling match. □ *Frank spelled everyone else down and won the spelling bee.*

spell something **out**† **1.** *Lit.* to spell something (with letters). □ *I can't understand your name. Can you spell it out?* □ *Please spell out all the strange words so I can write them down correctly.* **2.** *Fig.* to give all the details of something. □ *I want you to understand this completely, so I'm going to spell it out very carefully.*

spew something **out**† to have something gush forth. □ *The faucet spewed a little yellowish water out and stopped altogether.*

spew something **up**† to gush something upward. □ *The geyser spewed hot water and steam up every hour on the hour.*

spice something **up**† **1.** *Lit.* to make some food or drink more spicy. □ *Judy spiced the cider up by adding cinnamon and nutmeg.* □ *She spiced up the chili too much.* **2.** *Fig.* to make something more interesting, lively, or sexy. □ *I'm afraid that the nude scenes spiced the musical up too much. Some people walked out.* □ *Judy liked to spice her lectures up by telling jokes.* □ *She spiced up each lecture with a joke.*

spiel something **off**† to recite a list of things very rapidly; to recite something very rapidly. □ *I used to be able to spiel the names of the presidents off.*

spiff something **up**† to polish and groom something very well; to make something clean and tidy. □ *See if you can spiff this place up a little.*

spill over 1. [for a container] to overflow. □ *I hope your bucket of water doesn't spill over.* □ *The milk glass spilled over because it was filled too full.* **2.** [for the contents of a container] to overflow. □ *The bucket is too full. I don't know why the water doesn't spill over.*

spin around 1. to turn around to face a different direction. □ *Jill spun around to face her accuser.* □ *Todd spun around in his chair so he could see who was talking to him.* **2.** to rotate, possibly a number of times. □ *The propellers spun around and soon the old plane began to taxi down the runway.*

spin off [for something] to part and fly away from something that is spinning; [for something] to detach or break loose from something. □ *The blade of the lawn mower spun off, but fortunately no one was injured.*

spin something **off**† **1.** *Lit.* [for something rotating] to release a part that flies away. □ *The propeller spun one of its blades off and then fell apart all together.* **2.** *Fig.* [for a business] to divest itself of one of its subparts. □ *The large company spun one of its smaller divisions off.* □ *It spun off a subsidiary and used the cash to pay down its debt.* **3.** *Fig.* [for an enterprise] to produce useful or profitable side effects or products. □ *We will be able to spin off a number of additional products.* □ *The development of this product will allow us to spin off dozens of smaller, innovative products for years to come.*

spin something **out**† to prolong something. □ *Was there really any need to spin the whole process out so long?*

spiral down to descend in a spiral path. □ *A path spiraled down and at the bottom was a small refreshment stand.*

spiral up to ascend in a spiral path. □ *The smoke spiraled up to the sky.*

spirit someone or something **away**† **(somewhere)** to sneak someone or something away to another place. □ *The police spirited the prisoner away before the crowd assembled in front of the jail.*

spirit someone or something **off**† **(to** some place) to hurry someone or something away, presumably unnoticed, to another place. □ *Aunt Jane spirited the children off to bed at half-past eight.*

spit something **out**† **1.** *Lit.* to cast something from the mouth. □ *The food was so terrible that I spit it out.* □ *I spit out the sweet potatoes.* **2.** *Fig.* to manage to say something. □ *Come on! Say it! Spit it out! Spit it out! Get it said!* **3.** *Fig.* to say something scornfully. □ *He spit out his words in utter derision.* □ *She spit out the most unpleasant string of curse words I have ever heard from anyone.*

spit something **up**† *Euph.* to vomit something. □ *Sally was afraid she was going to spit up her dinner.*

splash down [for a space capsule] to land in the water. □ *The capsule splashed down very close to the pickup ship.*

splash something **about** to scatter or slosh a liquid about. □ *Please don't splash that about. It will stain anything you spill it on.*

splay out to spread out; to extend out at an angle. □ *His feet splayed out so much that it was hard to see how he could stand up.* □ *The legs of the table splayed out and gave it sturdy support.*

splice something **together**† to connect things together, usually by twisting or tying a joint between the two. □ *I spent over an hour splicing the two ends of the ropes together, and it didn't hold for even a minute.*

split people up† to separate two or more people (from one another). □ *If you two don't stop chattering, I'll have to split you up.*

split someone or something **up**† (**into** something) to divide people or things up into something, such as groups. □ *I split up the class into two discussion sections.*

sponge someone or something **down**† to remove the [excess] moisture from someone or something; to wipe someone or something with a sponge. □ *The fight manager sponged his boxer down.*

sponge something **away**† to absorb, wipe up, and wipe away something, as with a sponge. □ *I will sponge away the mess.*

sponge something **up**† to absorb or take up moisture, as with a sponge. □ *I had to sponge the spilled milk up from the floor, the chair, the table, and the baby. What a mess!*

spoon something **out**† to serve something out, as with a spoon; to give something out, as with a spoon. □ *The cook spooned the beans out, giving plenty to each camper.*

spoon something **up**† to serve something that requires finding and bringing up out of a pot with a spoon. □ *The cook spooned the hard-cooked eggs up one by one.*

spout something **out**† **1.** *Lit.* to exude a liquid. □ *The hose spouted the cooling water out all over the children.* **2.** *Fig.* to blurt something out; to speak out suddenly, revealing some important piece of information. □ *She spouted the name of the secret agent out under the effects of the drug.* □ *She spouted out everything we wanted to know.*

sprawl out to spread oneself out casually while lounging. (Usually done one time, not habitually.) □ *He sprawled out and took up most of the space.*

spread out to separate and distribute over a wide area. □ *The sheriff told the members of the posse to spread out and continue their search.*

spread something **out**† to open, unfold, or lay something over a wider area. □ *Spread the wet papers out so they will dry.*

spring up to appear or develop suddenly; to sprout, as with a seedling. □ *We knew it was really spring when all the flowers sprang up.* □ *It seems as if the tulips sprang up overnight.*

sprout up to grow upward quickly, as do newly sprouted seedlings. □ *Many of the newly planted seeds failed to sprout up on time.*

spruce someone or something **up**† **1.** *Lit.* to tidy up and groom someone or something. □ *Laura's mother took a few minutes to spruce her daughter up for the party.* **2.** *Fig.* to refurbish or renew someone or something. □ *Do you think we should spruce this room up a little?*

spur someone **on**† to urge someone onward; to egg someone on. (*Fig.* on applying spurs to a horse.) □ *The crowd spurred the runners on throughout the race.*

sputter out [for a flame] to go out in little puffs. □ *The fire sputtered out after midnight and we all got very cold before dawn.*

squander something **away**† to waste something; to use up something valuable wastefully. □ *Where is all the money I gave you last month? Did you squander it all away?*

square someone **away**† to get someone or something arranged or properly taken care of. □ *See if you can square Bob away in his new office.*

square something **off**† to make something square; to trim something until it is square. □ *You will have to square this corner off a bit so it will match the part it will be attached to.*

square something **up**† to cause something to have right angles. □ *Please square the door frames up better before you nail them in.*

squash someone or something **up**† to grind someone or something up; to mash someone or something up. □ *You had better stay out of the traffic, or some big truck will squash you up!*

squash something **down**† to crush something down; to pack something down. □ *Squash the ice cream down so the air will be pushed out.*

squash something **in**† to crush or make something concave by squashing or mashing. □ *The children squashed the Halloween jack-o'-lantern in and ruined it.*

squeeze someone or something **up**† to press people or things close together. □ *The usher tried to squeeze us up so she could seat more people.*

squirrel something **away**† *Fig.* to hide something or store something in the way that a squirrel stores nuts for use in the winter. □ *I squirreled a little money away for an occasion such as this.*

stack something **up**† to make a stack of things. (Also without the *up*.) □ *Where should I stack them up?*

stack up [for something] to accumulate, as in stacks. □ *Your work is stacking up. You will have to work late to finish it.*

stagger around to go about tottering or wobbling, especially as if drunk. □ *The wounded man staggered around and then fell.*

stake someone or something **out**† **1.** to position a person so that someone or something can be observed or followed. □ *The cops staked the car out and made the arrest.* □ *Barlowe staked out the apartment building and watched patiently for an hour.* **2.** to position a person to observe someone or something. □ *He staked his best operative out in front of the building.*

stake something **off**† to mark out the boundaries of an area of land with stakes. □ *The prospectors staked an area off for themselves.*

stall someone or something **off**† to put off or delay someone or something. □ *The sheriff is at the door. I'll stall him off while you get out the back door.*

stammer something **out**† to manage to say something, but only haltingly. □ *Fred stammered the words out haltingly.*

stamp someone **out**† *Sl.* to get rid of or kill someone. (*Fig.* on stamp something out.) □ *You just can't stamp somebody out on your own!*

stamp something **out**† *Fig.* to eliminate something. □ *The doctors hope they can stamp cancer out.*

stand around to wait around, standing; to loiter. □ *Please don't stand around. Get busy!*

stand aside 1. *Lit.* to step aside; to get out of the way. □ *Please stand aside while the bridal party passes by.* □ *The guests stood aside while the bride and groom left.* **2.** *Fig.* to withdraw and ignore something; to remain passive while something happens. □ *He just stood aside and let his kids behave as they pleased.*

stand by to wait and remain ready. (Generally heard in communication, such as broadcasting, telephones, etc.) □ *Your transatlantic telephone call is almost ready. Please stand by.*

stand down 1. to step down, particularly from the witness stand in a courtroom. □ *The bailiff told the witness to stand down.* **2.** [for military forces] to move away from readiness for war. □ *After the peace treaty was signed, troops on both sides stood down.*

stand someone or something **off**† to repel the attack of someone or something; to defend against someone or something; to stave someone or something off. □ *It was all we could do to stand them off.*

stand someone **up**† **1.** to place someone into a standing position. □ *I tried to stand him up, but he was just too tired.* □ *Let's try to stand up Timmy and get him awake.* **2.** to fail to show up for a meeting or a date. □ *He stood her up once too often, so she broke up with him.* □ *Tom stood up Mary once, and she never forgave him.*

stand together 1. to stand in a group. □ *All the members of the family stood together for a photograph.* □ *Please stand together so I can count you.* **2.** to remain united. □ *We must stand together if we want to defeat this enemy.*

stand up 1. to arise from a sitting or reclining position. □ *He stood up and looked across the valley.* □ *She had been sitting for so long that it was a pleasure to stand up.* **2.** to be in a standing position. □ *I stood up throughout the whole trip because there were no more seats on the train.* **3.** to wear well; to remain sound and intact. □ *This material just doesn't stand up well when it's washed.* □ *Her work doesn't stand up under close scru-*

tiny. **4.** [for an assertion] to remain believable. □ *His testimony will not stand up in court.*

stare someone **down**† to pressure someone to capitulate, back down, or yield by staring. □ *Don't try to stare me down. I have nerves of steel.*

start off to begin; to set out on a journey. □ *We will start off as soon as we can get everything packed.*

start over to begin again. □ *I have messed this up so much that there is nothing to do now but start over.*

start someone **over** to cause someone to begin again; to lead someone to begin again. □ *The orchestra messed up the first few bars, so the conductor started them over again.*

start something **up**† to start something, such as a car or some procedure. (Also without *up*.) □ *It was cold, but I managed to start up the car without any difficulty.*

start up to begin; to begin running, as with an engine. □ *The car started up without a problem.*

stash something **away**† to hide something; to set something aside for use at a later time. □ *Please stash this away somewhere. You may need it someday.*

stave someone or something **off**† to hold someone or something off; to defend against the attack of someone or something. □ *The citizen was not able to stave the mugger off.*

stave something **in**† to crush something in. (The past tense is usually *stove* with ships, and otherwise, *staved*.) □ *The rocks on the reef staved the hull of the ship in.*

stay behind [for someone] to remain in a place when others have left. □ *I will stay behind and tell the late arrivers where you have gone.*

stay down to remain in a prone, squatting, or sitting position. □ *Stay down until the danger is over.*

steam someone **up**† **1.** *Sl.* to get someone excited. □ *Steam yourselves up and get in there and win this game!* **2.** *Sl.* to get someone angry. □ *This whole mess steamed me up but good.*

steam something **up**† to cause something to be covered with water vapor due to the presence of steam. □ *Our breaths steamed the windows up.*

steam up 1. *Lit.* to become covered with a film of steam or water vapor. □ *The windows steamed up and we had to wipe them so we could see out.* **2.** to drink heavily; to get drunk. □ *Fred and Mike were steaming up in the back room.*

step off to come off something by taking a step. □ *She came to the bottom step and stepped off.*

step something **down**† to reduce the intensity or amount of something by one step or grade. □ *See if you can step the lights down a little.*

step something **up**† **1.** to make something more active. □ *I hope we can step the pace of business up in the next few days.* **2.** to make something go or run faster. □ *The engineer stepped the motors up and the production line moved even faster.*

step up to increase. □ *Industrial production stepped up a large amount this last quarter.*

stick around [for a person] to remain in a place. □ *Oh, Ann. Please stick around for a while. I want to talk to you later.*

stick out to project outward. □ *You can't lock your suitcase because there is a bit of cloth sticking out.*

stick someone or something **up**† to rob someone or a business establishment. (Presumably with the aid of a gun.) □ *Max tried to stick the drugstore up.*

stick something **down**† to fasten something down, as with glue or paste. □ *Get some glue and stick down this wallpaper, please.*

stick something **out**† to endure something; to stay with something. (The *something* can be vaguely expressed using *it*.) □ *I will stick it out as long as I can.*

stick something **together 1.** to glue or paste something together. □ *Use glue to stick these pieces together.* □ *Please stick the pieces of the broken vase together with glue.* **2.** to assemble something, perhaps in haste. □ *He just stuck the model plane together, making a mess of it.*

stick something **up**† **1.** to fasten something to a place where it can be seen; to put something on display, especially by gluing, tacking, or stapling. □ *Stick this notice up. Put a copy on every bulletin board.* **2.** to raise something; to hold something up. □ *She stuck her hand up because she knew the answer.*

stick together 1. *Lit.* to adhere to one another. □ *The noodles are sticking together. What shall I do?* □ *You need to keep the pieces separate while you fry them or else they will stick together.* **2.** *Fig.* to remain in one another's company. □ *Let us stick together so we don't get lost.* □ *They stuck together through thick and thin.*

stick up to stand upright or on end; to thrust upward. □ *The ugly red flower stuck up from the bouquet.* □ *Why is the worst-looking flower sticking up above all the rest?*

stiffen something **up**† to make something rigid or tense. □ *He added a little starch to the rinse water to stiffen his collars up a bit.*

stiffen up to become stiff. □ *The bread dough stiffened up as it got cold.* □ *My knees began to stiffen up after I sat still for an hour.*

stink something **up**† to make something or some place smell very bad. □ *The rotten eggs will stink up the whole house.*

stir someone **up**† *Fig.* to get someone excited; to get someone angry. □ *The march music really stirred the audience up.* □ *The march stirred up the audience.*

stir something **into** something AND **stir** something **in**† to mix something into something. □ *The painter stirred too much red pigment into the paint.*

stir something **up**† **1.** *Lit.* to mix something by stirring. □ *Please stir the pancake batter up before you use it.* **2.** *Fig.* to cause trouble. □ *Why are you always trying to stir trouble up?*

stitch something **up**† to sew something together; to mend a tear or ripped seam. □ *I tore my shirt. Would you stitch it up, please?*

stoop down to dip, duck, or squat down. □ *I had to stoop down to enter the tiny door.*

stoop over to bend over. □ *As he stooped over, he lost his balance and fell.*

store something **away**† to put something away for future use; to set something aside. □ *Store the extra rice away for use next week.*

store something **up**† to build up and lay away a supply of something. □ *The bears will store fat up for the long winter.*

stow away to conceal oneself in a vehicle, originally a ship, in order to travel without paying. □ *Don got to this country by stowing away on a cargo ship.*

stow something **away**† to pack something away. □ *I have to stow my clothes away before I go to bed.* □ *Please stow away your things and get right to work.*

straighten out 1. to become straight. □ *The road finally straightened out.* **2.** to improve one's behavior or attitude. □ *I hope he straightens out before he gets himself into real trouble.*

straighten someone **out**† **1.** to make someone's body straight or orderly. □ *The undertaker straightened Sam out in his coffin.* **2.** to cause someone to behave better or to have a better attitude; to reform someone. □ *You are terrible. Someone is going to have to straighten you out!* **3.** to help someone become less confused about something. □ *Can you straighten me out on this matter?*

straighten something **out**† **1.** to make something straighter. □ *Please straighten out this line of people.* **2.** to bring order to something that is disorderly. □ *See if you can straighten this mess out.*

straighten up 1. to sit or stand more straight. □ *Billy's mother told him to straighten up or he'd fall out of his chair.* **2.** to behave better. □ *Bill was acting badly for a while; then he straightened up.*

strap someone or something **down**† to tie or bind someone or something down to something. □ *The nurses strapped Gary down in preparation for the operation.*

stretch out [for one] to extend and stretch one's body to its full length. □ *I need a bigger bed. I can't stretch out in this one.*

stretch something **out**[†] **(to** someone or something**)** to reach something out to someone or something. □ *Jeff stretched his hand out to Tiffany.*

strike out 1. *Lit.* [for a baseball batter] to be declared out after making three strikes. (Baseball.) □ *And so Drew Wilson strikes out for his second time in this game!* **2.** *Fig.* to fail. □ *Well, we struck out again, but we'll keep trying.* □ *I hear you struck out on that Acme proposal. Better luck next time.*

strike someone or something **down**[†] to knock someone or something down by striking. □ *Max struck Lefty down with one blow.*

strike something **down**[†] [for a court] to invalidate a ruling or law. □ *The higher court struck the ruling of the lower court down.*

strike something **out**[†] to cross something out of a section of printing or writing. □ *This is wrong. Please strike it out.*

strike something **up**[†] to begin something; to cause something to begin. (Typically, the playing of a band, a conversation, or a friendship.) □ *We tried to strike a conversation up—to no avail.*

string someone **along** to maintain someone's attention or interest, probably insincerely. □ *You are just stringing me along because you like to borrow my car. You are not a real friend.*

string someone **up**[†] to hang someone. □ *The sheriff swore he would string Tex up whenever he caught him.*

string something **out**[†] **1.** *Lit.* to unwind, stretch, or straighten something, such as wire, and extend it. □ *The workers strung the wires out before installing them.* **2.** *Fig.* to cause something to take more time than it ought to. □ *Is there any good reason to string this meeting out any longer?*

strip down to remove one's clothing. □ *The doctor told Joe to strip down for his examination.*

stub something **out**† to put out something, such as a cigarette or cigar, by crushing the burning end against a hard object. □ *Max stubbed his cigar out and tossed it into the street.*

stuff something **up**† to plug something by stuffing something in its opening. □ *He stuffed the hole up with old newspapers.*

suck someone **in**† AND **take** someone **in**† to deceive someone. □ *I think that someone sucked in both of them. I don't know why they bought this car.*

suck someone or something **down**† [for a vacuum or water currents] to pull someone or something downward. □ *The savage currents sucked the swimmers down to their death.*

suck someone or something **under** [for a current or waves] to pull someone or something beneath the surface of the water. □ *The strong rip tide almost sucked me under!* □ *It almost sucked our boat under.*

suck something **in**† **1.** *Lit.* to draw something into one's mouth by sucking. □ *She sucked the milk shake in so hard she nearly collapsed the straw.* **2.** *Fig.* to draw in one's belly, gut, or stomach. □ *Suck that belly in!*

suck something **up**† to pick something up by suction, as with a vacuum cleaner, or through a straw. □ *Will this vacuum suck all this dirt up?*

suit (oneself) up to get into one's uniform, especially an athletic uniform. □ *The coach told the team to suit up for the game by three o'clock.*

sum (something) up[†] to give a summary of something. □ *I would like to sum this lecture up by listing the main points I have covered.* □ *It is time for me to sum up.*

summon something **up**[†] to call forth particular qualities, such as strength, courage, wisdom, etc. □ *She summoned her courage up and went into the room.*

surge out (of something**)** to burst forth or gush out of something or some place. □ *The water surged out of the huge crack in the dam.*

surge up to rush or gush upwards. □ *A spring of fresh water surged up under the stone and flowed out on the ground.*

swab something **down**[†] to wash or scrub something, such as the deck of a ship. □ *The sailors were told to swab the deck down each day.*

swab something **out**[†] to wash or wipe something out in order to make it clean. □ *The doctor swabbed my ear out carefully.*

swallow someone or something **up**[†] **1.** *Lit.* to eat or gobble up someone or something. □ *The fairy-tale wolf threatened to swallow the pig up in one bite.* **2.** *Fig.* to engulf or contain something. □ *The vast garage seemed to swallow the cars up.*

swallow something **down**[†] to swallow something. □ *Here, take this pill and swallow it down.*

sweat something **off**[†] *Fig.* to get rid of excess fat or weight by exercising or taking a steam bath to produce sweat. □ *I think I can sweat a lot of this fat off.*

sweep someone or something away

sweat something **out**† **1.** *Lit.* to get rid of something in one's body by sweating. □ *I have a bit of a cold, and I am going to try to sweat it out.* **2.** *Fig.* to endure something unpleasant. □ *It was an ordeal, but I sweated it out.* **3.** *Fig.* to endure suspense about something. □ *She sweated the two-hour wait out until she heard the results of her bar exams.*

sweep along to glide along smoothly, as if flying. □ *The fallen leaves blew up against the fence, swept along by a strong wind.*

sweep someone or something **aside**† to push or brush someone or something aside. □ *The guards swept the spectators aside as the king's coach approached.*

sweep someone or something **away**† to dispose of someone or something by pushing or brushing away. □ *The waves nearly swept us away.*

sweep something **down**† to clean something by sweeping. □ *Please sweep this floor down whenever you make a mess here.*

sweep something **out**† to clean something out by sweeping. □ *Someone has to sweep the garage out.*

sweep something **under the carpet 1.** *Lit.* to hide dirt by brushing it away under the edge of a carpet. □ *He was in such a hurry with the cleaning that he just swept the dirt under the carpet.* **2.** *Fig.* to hide or ignore something. □ *You made a mistake that you can't sweep under the carpet.*

sweep something **up**† **1.** *Lit.* to clean up and remove something, such as dirt, by sweeping. □ *Please sweep these crumbs up.* □ *Can you sweep up these crumbs?* **2.** *Lit.* to clean up some place by sweeping. □ *Please sweep this room up.* **3.** *Fig.* to arrange something, such as hair, into a curve or wave. □ *The hairstylist swept her hair up over the top. No one liked it.*

sweep up to clean up by sweeping. □ *Please give me a few minutes to sweep up before you come to visit.*

sweeten someone **up**† to make someone more pleasant. □ *I had hoped that a week in the Caribbean would sweeten him up.*

sweeten something **up**† to make something taste sweeter. □ *Where is the sugar? I need to sweeten this up a little.*

swell out to bulge outward; to expand outward. □ *The west wall of the garage swelled out just before the building collapsed.*

swell up to enlarge; to inflate; to bulge out. □ *I struck my thumb with a hammer and it swelled up something awful.*

swirl around [for dust or a fluid] to circle around. □ *The liquid swirled around in the flask as Toby shook it up.*

switch off 1. *Lit.* [for something] to turn itself off. □ *At midnight, all the lights switched off automatically.* **2.** *Fig.* [for someone] to stop paying attention; to become oblivious to everything. □ *I got tired of listening and switched off.*

switch on 1. [for something] to turn itself on. □ *Exactly at midnight, the lights switched on.* □ *The radio switched on early in the morning to wake us up.* **2.** *Sl.* [for someone] to become alert or excited. □ *The wild music made all the kids switch on and start to dance.*

switch someone or something **off**† to cause someone or something to be quiet or stop doing something. □ *I got tired of listening to her, so I punched the button and switched her off.*

switch something **on**† to close an electrical circuit that causes something to start functioning or operating. □ *Please switch the fan on.*

switch something **out**† to remove something from an electrical circuit to turn it off. □ *Please switch the light out.* □ *I switched out the light.*

T

tack something **down**† to fasten something down with small nails. □ *Someone had better tack this carpet down.*

tack something **up**† to fasten something onto something with tacks. □ *The drapes started to fall, so we tacked them up again.*

tag someone **out**† [in baseball] to touch with the ball, and thereby put someone out. □ *The shortstop tagged the runner out and retired the side.*

take off 1. *Fig.* to leave the ground and begin to fly. (As with a bird or an airplane.) □ *When do we take off?* □ *The eagle took off and headed toward the mountains.* **2.** *Fig.* [for someone] to leave in a hurry. □ *She really took off from there quickly.* □ *I've got to take off—I'm late.* **3.** *Fig.* [for something] to start selling well. □ *The fluffy dog dolls began to take off, and we sold out the lot.* **4.** *Fig.* to become active and exciting. □ *Did the party ever take off, or was it dull all night?*

take someone **apart**† **1.** *Sl.* to beat someone up. □ *Don't talk to me that way, or I'll take you apart.* **2.** *Inf.* to criticize or defame someone or something. □ *They really took me apart, but I just ignore bad reviews.*

take someone **around**† to show someone the premises; to introduce someone to the people on the premises. □ *Mr. Franklin needs a plant tour. Would you take him around?*

take someone **aside**† to remove someone temporarily from the group for the purposes of discussing something privately. □ *I'm sorry he insulted you. I'll take him aside and talk to him about it.*

take someone **off**† *Sl.* to kill someone. (Underworld.) □ *Barlowe didn't want to have to take off Lefty, but he was afraid he might talk.*

take someone **on 1.** to enter into a fight or argument with someone. □ *I pretended to agree because I really didn't want to take him on.* **2.** to employ someone. □ *I think we could take you on as an assistant editor, but it doesn't pay very well.*

take someone or an animal **in**† to provide shelter for someone or an animal. □ *When I needed a place to live, my uncle took me in.*

take someone or something **down**† to move someone or something to a lower position or level. □ *The boss is downstairs and wants to meet our visitor. Will you take her down?* □ *The way down to the lobby is confusing. Let me take down our visitor.*

take someone or something **on**† to accept the task of handling a difficult person or thing. □ *Nobody wanted to take on Mrs. Franklin, but it had to be done.*

take someone **out**† **1.** to date someone. □ *I hope he'll take me out soon.* □ *She wanted to take out her guest for the evening.* **2.** to block out a player in football. □ *You take Joe out and I'll carry the ball.* □ *Who was supposed to take out that huge guy?* **3.** *Sl.* to kill someone. (Underworld.) □ *Mr. Gutman told Lefty to take Max out.*

take someone **up**† to discuss or deal with someone. (See also **take** something **up**.) □ *What are we going to do about*

Bill? Are we going to take Bill up today at the board meeting?

take something **apart**† **1.** *Lit.* to disassemble something. □ *Bobby took his bicycle apart.* □ *You take apart everything that is mechanical.* **2.** *Fig.* to damage or ruin something. □ *The wreck took both cars apart.* □ *The high wind took apart the roof and the fence.* **3.** *Fig.* to criticize something severely. □ *The critic took the play apart.*

take something **back**† to retract a statement; to rescind one's remark. □ *You had better take back what you said about my sister.*

take something **down**† **1.** to take some large or complicated things apart. □ *They plan to take all these buildings down and turn the land into a park.* **2.** to write something down in something. □ *Please take these figures down in your notebook.*

take something **in**† **1.** to reduce the size of a garment. □ *This is too big. I'll have to take it in around the waist.* **2.** to view and study something; to attend something involving viewing. □ *The mountains are so beautiful! I need an hour or so to take it all in.* □ *I want to sit here a minute and take in the view.* □ *Would you like to take in a movie?* **3.** to receive money as payment or proceeds. □ *How much did we take in today?* □ *The box office took nearly a thousand dollars in within just the last hour.* **4.** to receive something into the mind, usually visually. □ *Could you take those explanations in? I couldn't.* □ *I could hardly take in everything she said.* **5.** to inhale, drink, or eat something. □ *I think I'll go for a walk and take some fresh air in.*

take something **off**† to remove something, such as an article of clothing. □ *Please take your coat off and stay a while.*

take something **out**† **1.** *Lit.* to carry something outside. □ *Please take the trash out.* □ *I'll take out the trash.* **2.** *Inf.* to bomb or destroy something. □ *The enemy took out one of the trucks, but not the one carrying the medicine.*

take something **over**† **1.** to assume responsibility for a task. □ *It looks as if I'm going to have to take the project over.* □ *I will take over the project.* **2.** to acquire all of an asset; [for a company] to acquire another company. □ *Carl set out to take the failing airline over.* **3.** to take control of something. □ *The dictator hoped to take over the world little by little.*

take something **up**† **1.** [for someone or a group] to deliberate something. □ *When will the board of directors take this up?* **2.** to raise something, such as the height of a hem. □ *The skirt is too long. I'll have to take it up.* **3.** to continue with something after an interruption. □ *They took it up where they left off.* □ *Let's take up this matter at the point we were at when we were interrupted.* **4.** to begin something; to start to acquire a skill in something. □ *When did you take this hobby up?* □ *I took up skiing last fall.* **5.** to absorb something. □ *This old sponge doesn't take much water up.* **6.** to adopt something new. □ *I see you've taken a new lifestyle up.*

take the slack up† **1.** *Lit.* to tighten a rope that is holding something loosely. □ *Take the slack up if you can.* □ *This clothesline is too loose. Do something to take up the slack.* **2.** *Fig.* to do what needs to be done; to do what has been left undone. □ *Do I have to take the slack up?*

talk someone **down**[†] **1.** to win at debating someone. □ *Liz was able to talk her opponent down.* □ *She talked down her opponent.* **2.** to direct a novice pilot to make a safe landing by giving spoken instructions over the airplane's radio. □ *The people on the ground talked down the amateur pilot successfully.* **3.** to convince someone to lower the price of something. □ *The price tag said $2,000 for the car, but I talked down the salesman by threatening to go elsewhere.*

talk someone or something **over**[†] **(with** someone**)** to discuss someone or something with someone. □ *I want to talk John over with my staff.* □ *I will talk over this matter with Sam.*

talk someone or something **up**[†] to promote or speak in support of someone or something. □ *I've been talking the party up all day, trying to get people to come.* □ *They keep talking up the candidate as if he represented a real change.*

talk something **out**[†] to settle something by discussion. □ *Let's not get mad. Let's just talk it out.*

talk something **over**[†] to discuss something. □ *Come into my office so we can talk this over.*

talk something **through**[†] **1.** to discuss something in detail. □ *Let's talk the issue through and get it decided.* **2.** to get something approved by talking convincingly. □ *The board was reluctant to approve it, but I talked it through.*

talk something **up**[†] to promote or advertise something by saying good things about it to as many people as possible. □ *Let's talk the play up around campus so we can get a good audience.*

tally something **up**[†] to add something up. □ *Please tally everything up and tell me the total.*

tear someone apart (sense 2)

tamp something **down**† to pat or pack something down.
□ *Tamp the soil down over the seeds after you plant them.*

tear along to go along very fast, as in running, driving, cycling, etc. □ *The cars tore along the road, raising dust and making noise.*

tear someone **apart**† **1.** *Lit.* to rip someone apart savagely. (See also **tear** something **apart**.) □ *Max threatened to tear Tom apart.* **2.** *Fig.* to cause two people, presumably lovers, to separate unwillingly. □ *The enormous disruption of the accident tore them apart and they separated.* □ *The bickering between their parents finally tore apart the engaged couple.* **3.** *Fig.* to cause someone enormous grief or emotional pain. □ *The death of her dog tore her apart.* **4.** *Fig.* to criticize someone mercilessly. □ *The critic tore apart the entire cast of the play.*

tear someone or something **down**† to criticize or degrade someone or something. □ *Tom is always tearing Jane* *down. I guess he doesn't like her.* □ *It's not nice to tear down the people who work in your office.*

tear someone **up**† *Fig.* to cause someone much grief. (See also **tear** someone **apart**.) □ *The news of Tom's death really tore Bill up.*

tear something **apart**† **1.** to pull or rip something apart. (See also **tear** someone **apart**.) □ *The bear tore the tent apart.* □ *The lions tore apart the wildebeest in minutes, and began eating it.* **2.** to criticize something mercilessly. □ *The critic tore apart the entire cast of the play.* **3.** to divide something or the members of a group, citizens of a country, etc. □ *The financial crisis tore the club apart.*

tear something **down**† to dismantle or destroy something. □ *They plan to tear the old building down and build a new one there.*

tear something **up**† to rip someone or something to pieces. □ *The two drunks tore the bar up in their brawling.*

tease something **out**† *Fig.* to separate threads or hairs by combing. □ *The hairdresser teased Jill's hair out carefully.*

tee off 1. *Lit.* to start the first hole in a game of golf. □ *It's time to tee off. Let's get on the course.* □ *What time do we tee off?* **2.** *Fig.* to begin [doing anything]; to be the first one to start something. □ *The master of ceremonies teed off with a few jokes and then introduced the first act.*

tell someone **off**† to scold someone; to attack someone verbally. (This has a sense of finality about it.) □ *I was so mad at Bob that I told him off.*

test something **out**† to try something out; to test something to see if it works. □ *I can't wait to test my new laptop out.*

thaw out to warm up from being frozen. □ *How long will it take for the chicken to thaw out?*

thaw someone or something **out**† to raise the temperature of someone or something above freezing; to warm someone up. □ *We need to get inside so I can thaw my brother out. His toes are almost frozen.*

thicken something **up**† **1.** to make something, such as a fluid, thicker. □ *I have to thicken this gravy up before we can serve dinner.* **2.** to make something wider. □ *See this line here? You need to thicken it up so that it shows more clearly.*

thin down to become thinner or slimmer. □ *He stopped eating desserts and fatty foods so he could thin down.*

thin someone **down**† to make someone thinner or slimmer. □ *What you need to thin you down is less, not more.*

thin something **down**† to dilute a fluid. □ *You should thin this down with a little water.* □ *Try to thin down this paint a little.*

thin something **out**† to make something less dense; to scatter something. □ *You will have to thin the young plants out, because there is not room for all of them.*

think something **out**† to think through something; to prepare a plan or scheme. □ *This is an interesting problem. I'll have to take some time and think it out.*

think something **over**† to think about something and whether one will choose to do it. □ *I need a few minutes to think it over.*

think something **through**† to run over and try to settle something in one's mind. □ *Let me think this through and call you in the morning.*

think something **up**† to contrive or invent something. □ *Don't worry. I'll find a way to do it. I can think something up in time to get it done.*

thrash something **out**† *Fig.* to discuss something thoroughly and solve any problems. □ *The committee took hours to thrash the whole matter out.*

throw someone **off** to interrupt and confuse someone; to mislead someone. □ *The interruption threw me off, and I lost my place in the speech.* □ *Little noises throw me off. Please try to be quiet.*

throw someone or something **around**† to toss or cast someone or something around. □ *The belligerent fellow at the bar threatened to throw me around a little if I didn't get out of his way.*

throw someone or something **aside**† **1.** *Lit.* to cast someone or something to the side. □ *He threw his child aside just as the car was about to run him down.* **2.** *Fig.* to get rid of someone or something. □ *He threw his wife aside and took up with a younger woman.*

throw someone **over** to end a romance with someone. □ *Jane threw Bill over. I think she met someone she likes better.*

throw something **away**† to toss something out; to dispose of something. □ *Should I throw this away?*

throw something **away**† **on** someone or something to waste something on someone or something. □ *I won't throw any more money away on your brother-in-law.*

throw something **back**† *Sl.* to eat or drink something quickly. □ *He threw a beer back and got up and left.*

throw something **down**† to cast something down onto the ground; to cast something to a lower level. □ *Dave took one look at the box and threw it down.*

throw something **up**† **1.** to build or erect something in a hurry. □ *They sure threw that building up in a hurry.* **2.** to vomit something. □ *He threw up his dinner.*

throw up to vomit. □ *I was afraid I would throw up, the food was so horrible.*

thrust out to stick out; to stab outward; to protrude outward. □ *A deck thrust out from the back of the house, offering a lovely view of the stream far below.*

thrust someone or something **aside**† to push someone or something out of the way or to one side. □ *Walter thrust Fred aside and dashed by him into the room.*

thrust something **down**† to jab something downward. □ *Max thrust the knife down and speared a piece of chicken.*

tidy something **up**† to clean something up; to make something more orderly. □ *Please tidy this room up.*

tie someone or something **up**† **1.** *Lit.* to bind someone or something securely. □ *The sheriff tied the crooks up and took them to a cell.* □ *I tied the package up and put a label on it.* **2.** *Fig.* to keep someone or something busy or occupied. □ *Sally tied up the photocopy machine all afternoon.*

tie something **back**† to bind or fasten something back out of the way. □ *George tied the curtains back to let a little more light in.*

tie something **off**† to tie the ends of something losing fluid, as blood vessels to prevent bleeding. □ *The surgeons* *tied all the blood vessels off—one by one—as they were exposed.*

tie something **up**† **1.** *Lit.* to tie strings or cords on something in order to close or contain it. □ *Please tie this package up securely so I can mail it.* □ *Tie up your shoes!* **2.** *Fig.* to conclude and finalize something. □ *Let's try to tie up this deal by Thursday.* **3.** *Fig.* to block or impede something, such as traffic or progress. □ *The stalled bus tied traffic up for over an hour.*

tie traffic up† *Fig.* to cause road traffic to stop. □ *If you tie traffic up for too long, you'll get a traffic ticket.*

tighten something **up**† to make something tighter. □ *Tighten your seat belt up. It looks loose.*

tighten up 1. *Lit.* [for something] to get tighter. □ *The door hinges began to tighten up, making the door hard to open and close.* **2.** *Fig.* [for someone or a group] to become miserly. □ *The government tightened up and our budget was slashed.* □ *We almost went out of business when we couldn't get credit because the bank tightened up.* **3.** *Fig.* [for someone or something] to become more restrictive. □ *The boss is tightening up on new hiring.*

tilt something **back**† to move something so it leans back. □ *Alice tilted her chair back and nearly fell over.*

time someone **in**† to record someone's arrival time. □ *I timed you in at noon. Where were you?*

time someone **out**† to record someone's departure time. □ *Harry had to time everyone out because the time clock was broken.*

tip someone **over** to cause someone to fall. □ *Oh! You almost tipped me over!*

tip something **over**† to cause something to fall over. □ *Did you tip this chair over?*

tip something **up**† to tilt something so it dumps. □ *Jason tipped the wheelbarrow up and dumped the dirt out.*

tire someone **out**† to exhaust someone. □ *Too much work will tire out the horses.*

toddle along 1. to walk along in an unconcerned manner. □ *Kathleen was just toddling along, minding her own business.* **2.** to walk away. □ *Why don't you toddle along now and let me get some work done?*

toddle away AND **toddle off** to walk away. □ *Not even noticing what had happened, the old lady got up and toddled away.* □ *Sam toddled away, leaving us behind to explain things to the boss.* □ *Wally toddled off, leaving his dinner untouched.* □ *Don't just toddle off when I'm talking to you!*

tone someone or something **up**† to make someone or something stronger or more fit, muscularly. □ *I suggested an exercise that would tone him up and make him feel better.* □ *The exercises toned up his tummy muscles.*

tone something **down**† to cause something to have less of an impact on the senses of sight or sound; to lessen the impact of something prepared for public performance or consumption. □ *This is rather shocking. You had better tone it down a bit.*

tool up to become equipped with tools. □ *The factory tooled up to make the new cars in only two weeks.*

tool something **up**† to equip a factory or production line with particular tools and machines, as for new products. □ *The manager closed down the factory so she could tool it up for the new models.*

top something **off**† to add to the difficulty of something. □ *I had a bad day, and to top it off, I have to go to a meeting tonight.*

topple over [for something very tall] to fall over. □ *I was afraid that Jimmy's stack of blocks would topple over.*

toss someone or something **around**† to throw someone or something around. □ *The waves tossed him around and almost dashed him on the rocks.*

toss someone or something **aside**† to throw someone or something aside or out of the way. □ *The kidnapper tossed the child aside and reached for his gun.* □ *The soldier tossed aside the helpless civilian and ran into the house.*

toss someone or something **away**† to throw someone or something away; to discard someone or something. □ *You can't just toss me away! I'm your husband!* □ *She tossed away her husband of twenty years.*

toss someone or something **back**† **1.** to throw or force someone or something backward. □ *The blast tossed me back into the room.* □ *The blast tossed back the emergency personnel.* **2.** to throw someone or something back to where someone or something came from. □ *My father always threatened to toss me back where I came from, the way a fish is returned to the water.*

toss something **around**† *Fig.* to discuss something. □ *I have a few things to discuss. Can we meet later and toss them around?*

toss something **off**† **1.** *Lit.* to throw something off (of oneself). □ *Tom tossed off his jacket and sat down to watch television.* **2.** *Fig.* to ignore or resist the bad effects of something. □ *John insulted Bob, but Bob just tossed it off.* □ *If I couldn't toss off insults, I'd be miserable.* **3.** *Fig.*

to produce something easily or quickly. □ *I tossed that article off in only an hour.* □ *Joe just tossed off a few words and left the room.* **4.** *Fig.* to drink a drink very quickly. □ *He tossed a few beers off and left.*

total something **up**† to add up the total of something. □ *Please total the bill up and let me see the cost.* □ *Total up the bill and give it to me.*

touch someone or something **off**† *Fig.* to ignite or excite someone or something; to excite anger or chaos. □ *She is very excitable. The slightest thing will touch her off.* □ *The appearance of the fox touched off a furor in the hen-house.*

touch something **up**† to fix up the minor flaws in something; to repair a paint job on something. □ *It's only a little scratch in the finish. We can touch it up easily.*

toughen someone or something **up**† to cause someone or something to be stronger, more uncompromising, or more severe. □ *A few days behind the service counter at the discount store will toughen her up quickly.* □ *Having to deal with complaints toughened up the clerk quickly.*

toughen up to become tougher, stronger, or more severe. □ *She will toughen up after a while. You have to be tough around here to survive.*

tow someone or something **away**† to pull something, such as a car or a boat, away with another car, boat, etc. (The *someone* refers to the property of someone, not the person.) □ *If I don't get back to my car, they will tow me away.* □ *The truck towed away my car.*

towel someone or something **down**† to rub someone or something dry with a towel. □ *The mother toweled her child down and dressed her in clean clothes.* □ *She toweled down the child gently.*

towel someone or something **off**† to dry someone or something with a towel. □ *The young mother toweled the baby off with a soft, warm towel.*

track something **up**† to mess something up by spreading around something dirty or messy with one's shoes or feet. □ *Please don't track the floor up!*

trade something **off**† **1.** *Lit.* to get rid of something in an exchange. □ *I traded my car off.* □ *I traded off my old car for a new one.* **2.** *Fig.* to sacrifice something in an exchange. □ *You may end up trading job security off for more money.*

trample someone or something **down**† to crush down someone or something with the feet. □ *Stay out of crowds at rock concerts. Those kids will trample you down if they get excited.*

trickle away [for a liquid] to seep or dribble away. □ *All the water trickled away down the drain.*

trigger someone **off**† to cause someone to become angry. □ *Your rude comments triggered her off.* □ *Your comments triggered off Bob's temper.*

trigger something **off**† to set something off, such as an explosion. □ *We were afraid that the sparks from the engine would trigger an explosion off.* □ *The sparks triggered off an explosion.*

trim (oneself) **down** to take action to become slimmer or lose weight. □ *I need to trim myself down before I go on vacation.* □ *I decided to trim down, but I never got around to it.*

trim something **away**† **(from** something**)** to cut something away (from something). □ *The butcher trimmed the fat away from the steak.*

trim something **down**† to reduce the size of something. □ *You will have to trim the picture down to get it into the frame.*

trip someone **up**† **1.** *Lit.* to cause someone to trip; to entangle someone's feet. (*Someone* includes *oneself.*) □ *The lines tripped up the crew.* **2.** *Fig.* to cause someone to falter while speaking, thinking, etc. □ *Mary came in while the speaker was talking and the distraction tripped him up.*

trot something **out**† *Fig.* to mention something regularly or habitually, without giving it much thought. (Fig. on the image of trotting out a pony for display.) □ *When James disagreed with Mary, she simply trotted her same old political arguments out.*

true something **up**† to straighten something up; to put something into true plumb. □ *Please true this door frame up better before you hang the door.*

trump something **up**† **1.** to promote or boost something. □ *They think they have to trump something up to get people to see it.* □ *They trumped up the movie so much that many people were disappointed when it finally came out.* **2.** to think something up; to contrive something. □ *Do you just sit around trumping charges up against innocent people?*

truss someone or something **up**† to bind, tie, or bundle someone or something up. □ *The attendants trussed Walter up and took him to a padded cell.* □ *They trussed up Walter tightly.*

try someone or something **out**† to test someone or something for a while; to sample the performance of someone or something. □ *We will try her out in the editorial department and see how she does.*

try something **out**† **on** someone to see how someone responds to something or some idea. □ *Let me try this idea out on you and see what you think.*

tuck something **away**† **1.** *Lit.* to hide or store something away. □ *Tuck this away where you can find it later.* □ *Can you tuck away this money somewhere?* **2.** *Fig.* to eat something. □ *The boys tucked away three pizzas and an apple pie.*

tuck something **up**† to raise up some part of one's clothing and attach it temporarily. □ *She tucked her skirt up and waded through the flooded basement.*

tucker someone **out** to tire someone out. □ *The heavy work tuckered the staff out early in the day.*

tumble down to fall down; to topple. □ *The old barn was so rickety that it almost tumbled down on its own.*

tune out *Fig.* to cease paying attention to anything at all. □ *I think that most of the audience tuned out during the last part of the lecture.*

tune someone or something **out**† to put someone or something out of one's consciousness; to cease paying attention to someone or something. □ *I had to tune the radio out in order to concentrate.*

tune something **in**† to adjust a radio or television set so that something can be received. □ *Could you tune the newscast in?*

tune something **up**† *Fig.* to adjust an engine to run the best and most efficiently. □ *You need to tune this engine up.* □ *Please tune up this engine so it will run more economically.*

225

tune up [for one or more musicians] to bring their instruments into tune. □ *You could hear the orchestra behind the curtain, tuning up.*

turn in 1. [for something] to fold or point inward. □ *Do my toes turn in too much?* □ *The legs of the table turned in at the bottom, giving a quaint appearance to the piece of furniture.* **2.** [for someone] to go to bed. □ *It's time to turn in. Good night.* □ *I want to turn in early tonight.*

turn off [for something] to go off; to switch off. □ *All the lights turn off automatically.*

turn on 1. *Lit.* [for something] to switch on and start running. □ *The lights turned on right at dusk.* **2.** *Fig.* to become interested or excited. □ *He turns on when he sees the mountains.*

turn over 1. *Lit.* to rotate so that the side that was on the bottom is now on top. □ *The turtle turned over and crawled away.* □ *She turned over to get some sun on her back.* **2.** AND **kick over** *Fig.* [for an engine] to start or to rotate. □ *My car engine was so cold that it wouldn't even turn over.* □ *The engine kicked over a few times and then stopped for good.* **3.** *Fig.* to undergo exchange; to be replaced. □ *The employees turn over pretty regularly in this department.*

turn someone **aside**† to divert someone from the flow of people. □ *The attendant turned aside all the persons who arrived late.*

turn someone **down**† to issue a refusal to someone. □ *We had to turn Joan down, even though her proposal was okay.*

turn someone **off**† to dull someone's interest in someone or something. □ *The boring prof turned me off to the subject.* □ *The preacher set out to turn off the congregation to sin.*

turn someone **on**† to excite or interest someone. □ *Fast music with a good beat turns me on.* □ *That stuff doesn't turn on anyone.*

turn someone **out**† **1.** *Lit.* to send someone out of somewhere. □ *I'm glad it's not winter. I'd hate to turn out someone in the snow.* **2.** *Fig.* to train or produce someone with certain skills or talents. □ *A committee accused the state university of turning out too many veterinarians.*

turn someone or something **back**† to cause someone or something to stop and go back; to cause someone or something to retreat. □ *They turned back the bus because the bridge was down.*

turn someone or something **in**† **(to** someone or something**)** to submit or refer someone or something to someone or a group, especially in some official capacity. □ *The good citizen turned his neighbor in for watering his lawn during the wrong hours.*

turn someone or something **over**† **to** someone or something to release or assign someone or something to someone or something; to transfer or deliver someone or something to someone or something. □ *The deputy turned the bank robber over to the sheriff.* □ *I turned over the money I found to the police.*

turn someone or something **up**† **1.** *Lit.* to increase the volume of a device emitting the sound of someone or something. □ *I can't hear the lecturer. Turn her up.* □ *Turn up the radio, please.* **2.** *Fig.* to discover or locate someone or something. □ *See if you can turn up any evidence for his presence on the night of January 16.* □ *Have you been able to turn up a date for Friday night?*

turn something **down**† **1.** to bend or fold something down. □ *Timmy had turned down his cuffs and caught one of them in his bicycle chain.* **2.** to decrease the volume of something. □ *Please turn the radio down.* **3.** to reject something; to deny someone's request. □ *The board turned our request down.*

turn something **off**† to switch something off so that it stops running or operating. □ *Please turn the light off.*

turn something **on**† to switch on something to make it run. □ *I turned the microwave oven on and cooked dinner.*

turn something **out**† **1.** to manufacture or produce something in numbers. □ *The factory turns out about seventy-five cars a day.* **2.** to turn off a light. □ *Please turn the hall light out.*

turn something **up**† **1.** to bend or fold something up. (See also **turn up**.) □ *Please turn your cuffs up. They are getting muddy.* **2.** to turn playing cards face-up. □ *Please turn all the cards up.*

turn up 1. [for part of something] to point upward. □ *The ends of the elf's funny little shoes turned up.* **2.** *Fig.* to happen. □ *Something always turns up to prevent their meeting.* **3.** *Fig.* to appear; to arrive and attend. □ *We'll send out invitations and see who turns up.*

twist up 1. to move upward in a twisting path. □ *The smoke twisted up into the sky.* □ *As the car twisted up the narrow path, we got a good view of the valley.* **2.** to become twisted.

type something **out**† to make some information presentable by typing or keying it. □ *Please type this out before you submit it to the board for approval.*

type something **up**† to type a handwritten document; to type a document, perhaps using a computer. □ *I will give this to you as soon as I type it up.*

U

urge someone **along** to encourage someone to continue or go faster. □ *We urged them along with much encouragement.*

urge someone **forward** to encourage someone to move forward. □ *The generals urged the troops forward.*

use someone **up** *Fig.* to use all the effort or talent a person has. □ *I used myself up. I'm done. I can't function anymore.*

use something **up**† to consume or use all of something. □ *Use the flour up. I have more in the cupboard.*

usher someone or something **into** some place AND **usher** someone or something **in**† to escort or lead a person, a group, or something into a place. □ *The guard ushered the group into the palace.*

usher someone or something **out of** some place AND **usher** someone or something **out**† to escort or lead someone or a group out of a place. □ *We ushered them from the room.*

V

vacuum something **out**† to clean an enclosed area out with a vacuum cleaner. □ *Can you vacuum out the car?*

vacuum something **up**† **(from** something**)** to clean something up from something with a vacuum cleaner. □ *He vacuumed up the birdseed from the kitchen floor.*

venture forth 1. *Fig.* to set out; to go forward; to go out cautiously. □ *George ventured forth into the night.* □ *I think I will venture forth. It looks safe.* **2.** *Fig.* to go forth bravely. □ *Let us venture forth and conquer the enemy.*

vomit something **out**† *Fig.* [for something] to spill forth a great deal of something. □ *The volcano vomited the lava out for days.*

vote someone or something **down**† to defeat someone or something in an election. □ *The community voted the proposal down.*

vote something **through**† to get something through a set of procedures by voting in favor of it. □ *They were not able to vote the bill through.*

W

wait something **out**[†] to wait until something ends. □ *I will wait the summer out, and if nothing happens, I'll write again.*

wake someone or an animal **up**[†] to cause someone or an animal to awaken. □ *Please don't wake me up until noon.*

wake up to awaken; to become alert. □ *Wake up! We have to get on the road.*

walk along to move along on foot. □ *I was just walking along when my heel broke off.*

walk off to walk away; to leave on foot abruptly. □ *She didn't even say good-bye. She just walked off.*

wall someone or something **in**[†] to contain someone or something behind or within a wall. (Implies a constriction of space, but not necessarily an inescapable area.) □ *The count walled his prisoner in permanently.* □ *Jane decided to wall in the little garden at the side of the house.*

wall someone or something **off**[†] to separate or segregate someone or something by building a wall. □ *She sat right across from me at her desk, listening to every phone call I made. Finally, the manager walled her off so we now can carry on our business in privacy.*

wall something **up**[†] **1.** to seal something up behind a wall. □ *We simply walled the old furnace up. It was cheaper than removing it.* **2.** to fill up an opening, such as a window or door, by building a wall. □ *We will have to hire someone to wall the doorway up.*

want someone or something **back** to desire the return of someone or something. □ *Timmy wanted his mother back very badly.*

warm someone or something **up**[†] to make someone or something warmer; to take the chill out of or off of someone or something. □ *I put him by the fire to warm him up a little.* □ *We warmed up our feet before the fire.*

warm someone **up**[†] **1.** to make someone warmer. □ *Stand by the fire and warm yourself up.* **2.** *Fig.* to help someone get physically prepared to perform in an athletic event. (As if exercising or loosening up someone's muscles.) □ *The referee told the coach to warm his team up so the game could begin.* □ *You have to warm up the team before a game.* □ *Be sure to warm yourself up before playing.* **3.** *Fig.* to prepare an audience for another—more famous—performer. (*Fig.* on ②.) □ *A singer came out to warm us up for the main attraction.*

warm up 1. [for the weather or a person] to become warmer or hotter. □ *I think it is going to warm up next week.* **2.** *Fig.* [for someone] to become more friendly. (A warm person is a friendly person.) □ *Todd began to warm up halfway through the conference.* **3.** AND **warm up for something** *Fig.* to prepare for some kind of performance or competition. □ *The team had to warm up before the game.*

warm something **over**[†] **1.** to reheat food to serve it as leftovers. □ *I'll just warm the rest over for lunch tomorrow.* □ *Jane warmed over yesterday's turkey.* **2.** *Fig.* to bring up a matter that was thought to have been settled. (*Fig.* on ①.) □ *Please don't warm that business over again. It is settled and should remain that way.*

warn someone **off**† to advise a person to stay away. □ *We placed a guard outside the door to warn people off until the gas leak could be fixed.*

wash away to be carried away by water or some other liquid. □ *The bridge washed away in the flood.*

wash out 1. *Inf.* to fail and be removed from something, such as school. □ *I don't want to wash out. It's my whole future.* **2.** *Inf.* to have a serious wreck. □ *The little car washed out on the curve.* □ *The vehicles have a tendency to wash out when cornering.* **3.** *Inf.* to lose a large amount of money. □ *Fred washed out on that stock deal.* □ *Lefty and Willie washed out at the racetrack.* **4.** *Inf.* to break down or collapse from exhaustion. □ *The whole play began to wash out during the second act. It was a lost cause by the third.*

wash someone or something **away**† [for a flood of water] to carry someone or something away. □ *The flood washed the boats away.*

wash someone or something **off**† to clean someone or something by washing. □ *She washed the muddy children off with a hose and put their clothes right into the washing machine.*

wash someone or something **up**† **1.** to clean up someone or something by washing. □ *Please wash the baby up as long as you are changing the diaper.* □ *Sam will wash himself up before dinner.* **2.** [for water or the waves] to bring someone or something up onto the shore or beach. □ *Look what the waves washed up! A bottle with a note in it!*

wash someone **out**† *Fig.* to deplete the strength or vitality of someone. □ *The flu really washed me out.* □ *The disease washed out the whole class.*

wash someone **up**† to terminate someone in something. □ *This error is going to wash you up as an account executive.* □ *Problems like this have washed up quite a few careers.*

wash something **away**† to clean something by scrubbing and flushing away the dirt. □ *Fresh water will wash the seawater away.*

wash something **out**† **1.** to wash out the inside of something; to wash something made of fabric. □ *I have to wash my socks out tonight.* □ *Wash the pitcher out before you put it away.* **2.** *Fig.* to rain on or flood an event so that it must be canceled. (Fig. on ①.) □ *Rain washed the game out.* □ *The storm washed out the picnic.* **3.** to wash or erode something out or away. □ *The flood washed the new bushes out.*

waste something **away**† to use something up wastefully; to dissipate something. □ *He wasted all his money away and had to live in poverty.*

water something **down**† **1.** to dilute something. □ *Who watered the orange juice down?* □ *Jim watered down the orange juice.* **2.** to water something thoroughly. □ *Water down the lawn this evening so it will grow tomorrow.* **3.** *Fig.* to reduce the effectiveness or force of something. (Fig. on ①.) □ *Please don't water my declaration down.*

wave someone or something **aside**† to make a signal with the hand for someone or something to move aside. □ *The police officer waved us aside and would not let us turn into our street.* □ *The officer waved aside the spectators.*

wave someone or something **off**† to make a signal with the hand for someone or something to remain at a distance. □ *There was someone standing in front of the bridge, waving everyone off. The bridge must have collapsed.*

wave someone or something **on**[†] to make a signal with the hand for someone or something to move on or keep moving. □ *The traffic cop waved us on.*

wave something **around**[†] to raise something up and move it around so that everyone can see it. □ *When Ruth found the money, she waved it around so everyone could see it.*

wear down *Fig.* to break down with wear; to erode. □ *The steps had worn down so much that each one was curved and slanted dangerously.*

wear off [for the effects of something] to become less; to stop gradually. □ *The effects of the painkiller wore off and my tooth began to hurt.*

wear out to become worn from use; to become diminished or useless from use. □ *My car engine is about to wear out.*

wear someone **down**[†] **1.** *Fig.* to exhaust someone. □ *This hot weather wears me down.* □ *The steamy weather wore down the tourists and made them stay in their hotels.* **2.** *Fig.* to reduce someone to submission or agreement by constant badgering. □ *Finally they wore me down and I told them what they wanted to know.*

wear someone **out**[†] *Fig.* to exhaust someone; to make someone tired. □ *If he wears out everybody on the team, nobody will be left to play in the game.*

wear something **away**[†] to erode something. □ *The constant rains wore the side of the cathedral away.*

wear something **down**[†] to grind something away; to erode something. □ *The constant rubbing of the door wore the carpet down.*

weigh someone down

wear something **out**† to make something worthless or non-functional from use. □ *I wore my shoes out in no time at all.*

weed someone or something **out**† *Fig.* to remove someone or something unwanted or undesirable from a group or collection. (*Fig.* on removing weeds from the soil.) □ *We had to weed the less productive workers out one by one.* □ *The auditions were held to weed out the actors with the least ability.*

weigh someone **down**† *Fig.* [for a thought] to worry or depress someone. □ *All these problems really weigh me down.*

weigh someone or something **down**† to burden someone or something. □ *The heavy burden weighed the poor donkey down.*

wet someone or something **down**† to put water onto someone or something. □ *Mother wet the children down with* a hose while she was washing the car. □ *Karen wet down the children with the hose.*

whack something **off**† **1.** *Sl.* to complete something easily or quickly. □ *If you want a pair of these, I can whack them off for you in a few minutes.* □ *The artisan whacked off a set of the earrings in a few minutes.* **2.** *Sl.* to cut or chop something off. □ *A tree branch is rubbing against the house. I guess I'll go out and whack that branch off.*

whack something **up**† *Sl.* to chop something up. □ *In about an hour, he had whacked the tree up into small logs.*

wheel someone or something **off**† to push or steer someone or something on wheels some distance away. □ *The nurse wheeled the old man off.* □ *Karen wheeled off the patient.*

whip around 1. to reverse suddenly. (As with the tip of a whip.) □ *A branch whipped around and tore my shirt.* **2.** to turn around very quickly and suddenly. □ *John whipped around when he heard the noise.*

whip someone or something **around**† to cause someone or something to reverse direction quickly. □ *The roller coaster whipped around the riders, right and left, until they were almost sick.*

whip something **off**† **1.** *Inf.* to do or create something quickly. □ *If you need another receipt, I can whip one off in a jiffy.* **2.** *Inf.* to remove something, such as an item of clothing, quickly. □ *He whipped the coat off and dived into the water.*

whip something **out**† **1.** *Inf.* to complete making or working on something quickly. □ *I think I can whip one out for you very quickly.* □ *The factory whips out twenty of these every minute.* **2.** *Inf.* to jerk something out [of some place]. □ *Liz whipped a pencil out of her pocket.*

...at someone or
...an't just wish him
...ve! □ *Don't try to wish*
...fe.

...g. to eat something very rapidly
...pieces. (As a wolf might eat.) □ *Liz*
...olf down her food.

...self **up** to allow oneself to become emotionally
...set. □ *Don't work yourself up over Sally. She's not worth it.*

work out 1. [for something] to turn out all right in the end. □ *Don't worry. Everything will work out.* **2.** [for someone] to do a program of exercise. □ *I work out at least twice a week.*

work someone or something **over**† to give someone or something a thorough examination or treatment. □ *The doctor really worked me over but couldn't find any-*

whip something **up**† to prepare, create, or put something together. □ *I haven't written my report yet, but I'll whip one up before the deadline.* □ *I will whip up the most beautiful arrangement you have ever seen.*

will something **away**† to give something away in a will. □ *The old man simply willed all his money away. He said he wouldn't need it when he was dead.*

win someone **over**† **(to** something**)** to succeed in making someone favorable to something. □ *I hope I can win them all over to our side.*

wind around someone or something to twist or coil ~ someone or something. □ *The ___ the rabbit, suffocating it.*

wind down to start runn~ *Things will begin to wind ___ mer.* □ *As things wind dow___*

wind someone **up 1.** *Inf. Fig.* t___ *That kind of music really winds ___* someone set to do a lot of talkir___ a clock.) □ *The excitement of th___ and she talked almost all night.*

wind something **down**† to slow somet___ something less hectic. □ *Let's wind t___ try to get people to go home. It's really___*

wind something **up**† **1.** *Lit.* to tighten the ___ thing, such as a watch or a clock. □ *Wina___ before you forget.* **2.** *Fig.* to conclude s___ *Today we'll wind that deal up with the ban___*

wipe out 1. *Inf.* to crash. □ *I wiped out on th___ The car wiped out on the curve.* **2.** *Inf.* to fall o___ from something, such as a bicycle, skates, a su___ a skateboard, etc. □ *If I wipe out again, my mo___*

wish someone or something away

wolf something down

wish someone or something **away**† to wish ___ something would go away. □ *You___ something. You'll have to ask him to le___ away. The difficulties of your___*

wolf something **down**† ___ and in very large ___ would never ___

work o___

___ attach ___ □ *We wired the* ___ *of the chimney.*

thing wrong. □ *They worked over the patient but found nothing.*

work someone **over**† **1.** to threaten, intimidate, or beat someone. □ *Walt threatened to work Sam over.* □ *Max had worked over Sam, and Sam knew that this was no idle threat.* **2.** to give someone's body a thorough examination or treatment. □ *The doctors worked her over to the tune of $1,500, but they couldn't find anything wrong with her.*

work someone **up**† to get someone ready for something, especially medical treatment. (See also **work oneself up**.) □ *The staff worked up three patients for surgery that morning.* □ *The doctor told the nurse to work Mr. Franklin up for surgery.*

work something **down**† to lower or reduce something, especially an amount of money. □ *Over a few months, they worked the price down, and the house soon was sold.*

work something **off**† **1.** *Lit.* to get rid of anger, anxiety, or energy by doing physical activity. □ *I was so mad! I went out and played basketball to work my anger off.* **2.** *Fig.* to pay off a debt through work rather than by money. □ *I had no money so I had to work the bill off by washing dishes.*

work something **out**† **(with** someone**)** to come to an agreement with someone; to figure out with someone a way to do something. □ *I think we can work this out with you so that all of us are satisfied.* □ *I will work out something with Karen.*

work something **over**† to rework something. □ *He saved the play by working the second act over.* □ *Would you work over this report and see if you can improve it?*

work something **up**† to prepare something, perhaps on short notice. □ *There are some special clients coming in this weekend. We need to make a presentation. Do you think you can work something up by then?*

work things out to improve one's state gradually by solving a series of problems. □ *If we sit down and talk this over, I am sure we can work things out.*

wrap something **up**† to complete work on something; to bring something to an end. □ *I will wrap the job this morning. I'll call you when I finish.*

wring something **out**† to squeeze or twist something dry of liquid. □ *He wrung the rag out and wiped up more of the spilled milk.*

wrinkle something **up**† to make something get wrinkles and creases. □ *I love the way you wrinkle your nose up.* □ *Don't wrinkle up your jacket.*

wrinkle up [for something] to draw up in wrinkles; [for something] to become wrinkled. □ *His nose wrinkled up as he smelled the burning pie.*

write someone **in**† (**on** something) to write the name of someone in a special place on a ballot, indicating a vote for the person. (Done when the person's name is not already printed on the ballot.) □ *Please write my name in on the ballot.*

write someone or something **off**† to drop someone or something from consideration. □ *I wrote off that piece of swampy land as worthless. It can't be used for anything.*

write someone or something **up**† to write an article about someone or something. □ *I wrote up a local business and sent the story to a magazine, but they didn't buy the story.*

write something **down**† to make a note of something; to record something in writing. □ *Please write this down.*

write something **off**† to absorb a debt or a loss in accounting. □ *The bill couldn't be collected, so we had to write it off.* □ *The bill was too large, and we couldn't write off the amount. We decided to sue.*

write something **off**† **(on** one's **taxes)** to deduct something from one's income taxes. □ *Can I write this off on my income taxes?* □ *I'll write off this trip on my taxes.*

write something **out**† **1.** to spell or write a number or an abbreviation. □ *Please write out all abbreviations, such as* Doctor *for* Dr. **2.** to put thoughts into writing, rather than keeping them in memory. □ *Let me write it out. Then I won't forget it.*

write something **up**† to prepare a bill, order, or statement. □ *Please write the order up and send me a copy.*

X someone or something **out**† to mark out something printed or in writing, with Xs. □ *Sally X'd the incorrect information out.* □ *Sally X'd out the incorrect information.* □ *You should X Tom out. He's not coming.*

X'd out 1. eliminated; crossed-out. □ *But the Babbits are X'd out.* □ *Put the X'd out Babbits back where they were.* **2.** *Sl.* killed. (Underworld.) □ *Mr. Big wanted Wilbur X'd out.* □ *He wanted Sam to see that all these punks were X'd out.*

Y

yank someone **around** *SL.* to harass someone; to give
someone a hard time. □ *Listen, I don't mean to yank you*
~und all the time, but we have to have the drawings by
~v. □ *Please stop yanking me around.*

~ or something **apart†** **1.** to pull, tear, or rip
~nething to pieces. □ *Please don't yank*
~ *He threatened to yank his opponent*
~eople or things. □ *The teacher*

~ip
~to
~' had
~)
~p your
□ *Zip*

~ory zone in
~and off for a

~dly.* □ *The bus*
~, I have to zoom off.
~lace. □ *A car zoomed*

~off something, such as
~er jacket off.

~ing up. □ *He*

Z

zero in (on someone or something**)** to aim directly at someone or something. □ The television camera zeroed in on the little boy scratching his head. □ The commercial zeroed in on the glass of cola.

zip something **on**† to put on a piece of clothing and zip it up. □ She zipped her jumper on and headed toward the door.

zip something **up**† **1.** to close a zipper. □ You should [zip] that zipper up. □ You should zip up that zipper. **2.** [to] close a garment by zipping a zipper closed. □ You [had] better zip your jacket up. □ You had better zip [up your] jacket. **3.** Sl. to close one's mouth. (Fig. on ②) [□] your mouth up, Fred!

zone something **off**† to create a special regulat[ed] an area. □ The council zoned part of the [ ] park.

zoom along to move along very rap[idly] zoomed along rapidly all night long.

zoom off to leave in a hurry. □ Sorr[y] [ ]

zoom up to drive or pull up to a [ ] up, and seven kids got out.